ARTISAN BREAD

in Five Minutes a Day

ARTISAN BREAD
in Five Minutes a Day

The Discovery That Revolutionizes Home Baking

JEFF HERTZBERG and ZOË FRANÇOIS

Photography by MARK LUINENBURG

ST. MARTIN'S PRESS ⚏ NEW YORK

THOMAS DUNNE BOOKS.
An imprint of St. Martin's Press.

ARTISAN BREAD IN FIVE MINUTES A DAY. Copyright © 2007 by Jeff Hertzberg and Zoë François.
All rights reserved. Printed in the United States of America. For information, address
St. Martin's Press, 175 Fifth Avenue, New York, N.Y. 10010.

www.thomasdunnebooks.com
www.stmartins.com

Design by Phil Mazzone

Photography © 2007 by Mark Luinenburg

Library of Congress Cataloging-in-Publication Data

Hertzberg, Jeff.
    Artisan bread in five minutes a day : the discovery that revolutionizes home baking / Jeff
Hertzberg and Zoë François.—1st ed.
        p. cm
    ISBN-13: 978-0-312-36291-1
    ISBN-10: 0-312-36291-9
    1. Bread.   I. François, Zoë.   II. Title.
    TX769.H474 2007
    641.8'15—dc22   2007027635

10

CONTENTS

ACKNOWLEDGMENTS

Cookbook deals for unknown authors without TV shows are a long shot these days. On top of that, we knew bread baking, but we didn't know publishing. So we needed some luck, and some generous people to help us. Our most heartfelt thanks go to Ruth Cavin, our risk-taking editor at St. Martin's Press, who heard us on the radio, liked our idea, and decided to publish us. Decisive is good. Otherwise this would still be just an eccentric family project. Lynne Rossetto Kasper took Jeff's call on her radio show, which gave us the opportunity to meet Ruth. Lynne also gave great advice and connected us with our top-notch literary agent, Jane Dystel.

We also had great friends and family to act as recipe testers. They baked endlessly and shared their criticism and praise with us. Once they started using our recipes, we understood that this would be a book for everyone—avid bakers and nonbakers alike. That was a revelation. So we owe our book to them: Allison Campbell, Alex Cohn, Ralph Cohn, Shelly Fling, Paul Gates (whose home was the first proving-ground), Ralph Gualtieri and Debora Villa (who carried our dough across international borders), Rachel Hertzberg and Julia Hertzberg (who proved that children could do our recipes), Jim and Theresa Murray, Lorraine Neal, Jennifer Sommerness, and Laura Silver. In addition to testing the breads, experienced editors Allison, Shelly, and Laura gave invaluable tips on the text itself. Thank you to Josh Manheimer, Dusti Kugler, Kelly Lainsbury,

Craig Neal, and Patricia Neal for lending their marketing expertise. Graham (Zoë's husband) gave immeasurable moral support and created our Web site, at www.artisanbreadinfive.com. And thanks to Fran Davis for allowing us to use nearly all the contents of her home as props for our photo shoots. Also thanks to Barb Davis for all of your support and to Laura Tiffany for opening your beautiful kitchen to us.

Gratitude to Zoë's colleagues from the culinary world who have served as mentors and shared their advice so generously: Stephen Durfee, Thomas Gumpel, Steven Brown, Raghavan Iyer, Suvir Saran, and Andrew Zimmern.

And enormous thanks to Mark Luinenburg, whose lush and beautiful photography enhances our book so much. Photo sessions at Mark's were as much fun as writing the book. Thanks for the gorgeous shots, and for helping us finish off all those carbs and coffee!

THE SECRET

Mix Enough Dough for Several Loaves and Store It in
the Refrigerator

It is so easy to have freshly baked bread when you want it with only five minutes a day of active effort. First, mix the ingredients from our recipe into a container all at once, and then let them sit for two hours. Now you are ready to shape and bake the bread, or you can refrigerate the dough and use it over the next couple of weeks. Yes, weeks! You've prepared enough dough for many loaves. When you want fresh-baked crusty bread, take a piece of the dough from the container and shape it into a loaf. Let it rise for twenty minutes or more and then bake. Your house will smell like a bakery and your family and friends will love you for it.

PREFACE

Early childhood music class may be one of the more unlikely places for co-authors to meet. I met Zoë amidst toddlers, circle games, and xylophones, and while the kids played, there was time for the grownups to talk. Zoë told me that she was a pastry chef and baker who'd been trained at the Culinary Institute of America (CIA).

What a fortuitous coincidence. I wasn't a food professional at all, but I'd been tinkering for years with easy methods for making homemade bread. We chatted about the challenges of re-creating authentic baguettes without French flour ("You can't? Uh, yeah, I knew that."). I told her about a recipe I'd been trying to develop for years to create artisan breads at home while investing very minimal time. The secret: use pre-mixed, high-moisture stored dough. It was promising, but it needed lots of work. This was a job for a professional baker.

I knew I had to get her to try the bread to convince her that she ought to join me in this project (and maybe more important, that involvement with five-minute yeast bread wouldn't turn her into a culinary laughingstock). This woman was a baker whose food at Minneapolis restaurants had been reviewed as "endlessly delicious...the best in town...appealing, inventive and flat-out gorgeous...." Maybe she had lower standards for bread than for dessert.

Luckily for me, she loved the bread, and she was willing to work on developing a book with me. And she had an idea for how to use the same approach to make pastries. Zoë created rich, sweet doughs from the basic recipe and turned them into a menu of fantastic dessert breads, pastries, rolls, and even doughnuts. I couldn't have anticipated this in a million years. I was startled at how easily stored yeast dough could be adapted for dessert (although Zoë knew all along that it would work).

I was trained as a scientist, not as a chef. That might have helped in developing a completely new process for homemade bread for amateurs, but I never could have brought the recipes to this level without the rigorous standards and creative repertoire of a professional. Our approach produces fantastic homemade loaves without the enormous time investment required in the traditional artisanal method.

On a lark, I called in to Lynne Rossetto Kasper's National Public Radio show *The Splendid Table* to get advice on getting our idea into print. Lynne gave great advice, but more important, a St. Martin's Press editor named Ruth Cavin, who'd been listening to Lynne's show, phoned *The Splendid Table*, contacted us, and asked for a book proposal. Zoë and I got busy writing one. The rest, as they say, is history.

Our goal in *Artisan Bread in Five Minutes a Day* is to help home bakers make great daily breads and pastries but still have a life outside the kitchen. And most important, for them to have fun while doing it. If you worry about the bread, it won't taste as good.

1

INTRODUCTION

❦

The Secret to Making Artisan Bread in Five Minutes a Day: Refrigerating Pre-Mixed Homemade Dough

Like most kids, my brother and I loved sweets, so dessert was our favorite time of day. We'd sit in the kitchen, devouring frosted supermarket doughnuts.

"Those are too sweet," my grandmother would say. "Me, I'd rather have a piece of good rye bread, with cheese on it."

Munch, munch, munch. Our mouths were full; we could not respond.

"It's better than cake," she'd say.

There's a certain solidarity among kids gorging on sweets, but secretly, I knew she was right. I could finish half a loaf of very fresh, very crisp rye bread by myself, with or without butter (unlike my grandmother, I considered cheese to be a distraction from perfect rye bread). The right stuff came from a little bakery on Horace Harding Boulevard in Queens. The shop itself was nondescript, but the breads were Eastern European masterpieces. The crust of the rye bread was crisp, thin, and caramelized brown. The interior crumb was moist and dense, chewy but never gummy, and bursting with tangy yeast, rye, and wheat flavors. It made great toast, too—and yes, it was better than cake.

The handmade bread was available all over New York City, and it wasn't a rarefied delicacy. Everyone knew what it was and took it for granted. It was not a stylish addition to affluent lifestyles; it was a simple comfort food brought here by modest immigrants.

I left New York in the late 1980s, and assumed that the corner bread shops would always be there, waiting for me, whenever I came back to visit. But I was wrong. As people lost interest in making a second stop after the supermarket just for bread, the shops gradually faded away. By 1990, the ubiquitous corner shops turning out great eastern, central, and southern European breads with crackling crusts were no longer so ubiquitous.

Great European breads, handmade by artisans, were still available, but they'd become part of the serious (and seriously expensive) food phenomenon that had swept the country. The bread bakery was no longer on every corner—now it was a destination. And nobody's grandmother would ever have paid six dollars for a loaf of bread.

I'd fly back to New York and wander the streets, bereft (well, not really). "My shop" on Horace Harding Boulevard had changed hands several times by 1990, and the bread, being made only once a day, was dry and didn't really have a lot of flavor. I even became convinced that we could get better bagels in Minneapolis—and from a chain store. Things were that grim.

So Zoë and I decided to do something about it. *Artisan Bread in Five Minutes a Day* is our attempt to help people re-create the great ethnic breads of years past, in their own homes, *without investing serious time in the process.* Using our straightforward, fast, and easy recipes, anyone will be able to create artisan bread and pastry at home with minimal equipment. Our first problem was: *Who has time to make bread every day?*

After years of experimentation, it turns out that *we* do, and with a method as fast as ours, you can, too. We solved the time problem *and* produced top-quality artisan loaves without a bread machine. We worked out the master recipes during busy years of career transition and starting families (our kids now delight in the pleasures of home-baked bread). Our lightning-fast method lets us find the time to bake great bread every day. We developed this method to re-capture the daily artisan bread experience without further crunching our limited time—and it works!

Traditional breads need a lot of attention, especially if you want to use a "starter" for that natural, tangy taste. Starters need to be cared for, with water and flour replenished from time to time. Dough needs to be kneaded until resilient, set to rise, punched down, allowed to rise again. There are boards and pans and utensils galore to be washed, some of which can't go into the dishwasher. Very few busy people can go through this every day, if ever. Even if your friends are all food fanatics, when was the last time you had homemade bread at a dinner party?

What about bread machines? The machines solve the time problem and turn out uniformly decent loaves, but unfortunately, the crust is soft and dull-flavored, and without tangy flavor in the crumb (unless you use and maintain time-consuming sourdough starter).

So we went to work. Over years, we found how to subtract the various steps that make the classic technique so time-consuming, and identified a few that couldn't be omitted.

And then, Zoë worked some pastry-chef magic: She figured out that we could use stored dough for desserts as well as for bread, applying the same ideas to sweet breads, rolls, and morning breads. It all came down to one fortuitous discovery:

Pre-mixed, pre-risen, high-moisture dough keeps well in the refrigerator.

This is the linchpin of *Artisan Bread in Five Minutes a Day*. By pre-mixing high-moisture dough (without kneading) and then storing it, daily bread baking becomes an easy activity; the only steps you do every day are shaping and baking. Other books have considered refrigerating dough, but only for a few days. Still others have omitted the kneading step, but none has tested the capacity of wet dough to be long-lived in your refrigerator. As our high-moisture dough ages, it takes on sourdough notes, reminiscent of the great European natural starters. When dough is mixed with adequate water (this dough is wetter than most you may have worked with), it can be stored in the refrigerator for up to two weeks (enriched or heavy doughs can't go that long but can be frozen instead). And kneading this kind of dough adds little to the overall product; you just don't have to do it. In fact, overhandling stored dough can limit the volume and rise that you get with our method. That, in a nutshell, is how you make artisan breads with the investment of only five minutes a day of active effort.

A one- or two-week supply of dough is made in advance and stored in the refrigerator. Measuring and mixing the dough takes less than 15 minutes. Kneading, as we've said, is not necessary. Every day, cut off a hunk of dough from the storage container and briefly shape it without kneading. Allow it to rest briefly on the counter and then toss it in the oven. We don't count the rest time (20 minutes or more depending on the recipe) or baking time (usually about 30 minutes) in our five-minute-a-day calculation since you can be doing something else while that's happening. If you bake after dinner, the bread will stay fresh for use the next day (higher-moisture breads stay fresh longer), but the method is so convenient that you probably will find you can cut off some dough and bake a loaf every morning, before your day starts. If you want to have one thing you do every day that is simply perfect, this is it!

Using high-moisture, pre-mixed, pre-risen dough makes most of the difficult, time-consuming, and demanding steps in traditional bread baking completely superfluous:

> ∽
>
> **Wetter is better:** The wetter dough, as you'll see, is fairly slack, and offers less resistance to yeast's expanding carbon dioxide bubbles. So, despite not being replenished with fresh flour and water like a proper sourdough starter, there is still adequate rise on the counter and in the oven.

1. You don't need to make fresh dough every day to have fresh bread every day: Stored dough makes wonderful fresh loaves. Only the shaping and baking steps are done daily, the rest has been done in advance.

2. You don't need a "sponge" or "starter": Traditional sourdough recipes require that you keep flour-water mixtures bubbling along in your refrigerator, with careful attention and replenishment. By storing the dough over two weeks, a subtle sourdough character gradually develops in our breads without needing to maintain sponges or starters in the refrigerator. With our dough-storage approach, your first loaf is not exactly the same as the last. It will become more complex in flavor as the dough ages.

3. It doesn't matter how you mix the dry and wet ingredients together: So long as the mixture is uniform, without any dry lumps of flour, it makes no difference whether you use a spoon, a high-capacity food processor, or a heavy-duty stand mixer. Choose based on your own convenience.

4. You don't need to "proof" yeast: Traditional recipes specify that yeast be dissolved in water (often with a little sugar) and allowed to sit for five minutes to prove that bubbles can form and the yeast is alive. But modern yeast simply doesn't fail if used before its expiration date and the baker remembers to use lukewarm, not hot water. The high-water content in our doughs further ensures that the yeast will fully hydrate and activate without a proofing step. Further storage gives it plenty of time to fully ferment the dough—our approach doesn't need the head start.

5. It isn't kneaded: The dough can be mixed and stored in the same resealable plastic container. No wooden board is required. There should be only one vessel to wash, plus a spoon (or a mixer). You'll never tell the difference between breads made with kneaded and unkneaded high-moisture dough, so long as you mix to a basically uniform

෨

What We *Don't* Have to Do: Steps from Traditional Artisan Baking That We Omitted

1. Mix a new batch of dough every time we want to make bread

2. "Proof" yeast

3. Knead dough

4. Cover formed loaves

5. Rest and rise the loaves in a draft-free location—it doesn't matter!

6. Fuss over doubling or tripling of dough volume

7. Punch down and re-rise

8. Poke rising loaves to be sure they've "proofed" by leaving indentations

Now you know why it only takes 5 minutes a day, not including resting and baking time.

୬୨

Start a morning batch before work, bake the first loaf before dinner: Here's a convenient way to get fresh bread on the table for dinner. Mix up a full batch of dough before breakfast and store it in the refrigerator. The lukewarm water you used to mix the dough will provide enough heat to allow the yeast to do its thing over the eight hours till you're home. When you walk in the door, cloak and shape the loaf and give it a quick rest, then bake as usual. Small loaves, and especially flatbreads, can be on the table in 40 minutes or less.

consistency. In our method, a very quick "cloaking and shaping" step substitutes for kneading (see Chapter 5, Step 5, page 28).

6. High-moisture stored dough can't over-rise accidentally: Remember that you're storing it long-term anyway. You'll see a brisk initial rise at room temperature over two hours; then the risen dough is refrigerated for use over the next week or two. But rising longer won't be harmful; there's lots of leeway in the initial rise time.

Given these simple principles, anyone can make artisan bread at home. We'll talk about what you'll need in Chapters 2 (Ingredients) and 3 (Equipment). You don't need a professional baker's kitchen. In Chapter 4, you'll learn the tips and techniques that we've taken years to accumulate. Then, in Chapter 5, we'll lay out the basics of our method, applying them to ordinary white dough and several delicious bread variations. Chapter 5's master recipe is the model for the rest of our recipes. We suggest you read it first and bake some of its breads before trying anything else. You won't regret it.

2

INGREDIENTS

∽

Here's a very practical guide to the ingredients we use to produce artisan loaves. Great breads really only require four basic ingredients: flour, water, yeast, and salt. The rest is detail.

Flours and Grains

Unbleached, white, all-purpose flour: This is the staple ingredient for most of the recipes in this book. We can't detect much taste difference among the national brands or the specialty products. In general, use what you like.

Unbleached all-purpose flour is our number-one choice because of its medium- (rather than high) protein content, which in wheat is almost all gluten. Gluten is the elastic protein that sets up a network of invisible microscopic strands, allowing bread dough to trap the carbon dioxide gas produced by bread yeast. Without gluten, bread won't rise. That's why flours that contain only minimal gluten (like rye) need to be mixed with wheat flour to make a successful loaf. Traditional bread recipes stress the need to "develop" gluten through kneading, which turns out *not* to be an important factor.

With a protein/gluten content at around 10 percent in most national brands, unbleached, all-purpose flour will have adequate protein to create a satisfying "chew" (a certain resistance to the teeth), but will have a low enough protein content to prevent heaviness, which can be a problem in high-moisture artisan baking.

Don't use bleached flour. We prefer unbleached flours for their natural creamy color, not to mention our preference for avoiding unnecessary chemicals. Even more important, bleaching removes some of the protein, and that throws off our recipes. If you use bleached flour, your dough will be too wet. And cake or pastry flours are far too low in protein (around 8 percent) to make successful high-moisture dough.

Bread flour: Bread flour has about 12 percent protein. If you prefer extra-chewy bread, you can substitute bread flour for all-purpose by decreasing the amount slightly (by about a quarter cup for every six cups of white all-purpose flour in the recipe). For some loaves that really need to hold their shape well (like *pain d'epi*), bread flour is preferred and we call for it in the recipe. Be aware that King Arthur All-Purpose Flour has a protein content of 12 to 13 percent, solidly in the range of high-protein bread flour rather than all-purpose.

Whole wheat flour: Whole wheat flour contains both the germ and bran of wheat; both of which are healthful and tasty. Together they add a slightly bitter, nutty flavor to bread that most people enjoy. The naturally occurring oils in wheat germ prevent formation of a crackling crust, so you're going for a different type of loaf when you start increasing the proportion of whole wheat flour. In general, you can use any kind of whole wheat flour that's available to you. Stone-ground whole wheat flour will be a bit coarser and more rustic. Most whole wheat flour labels will not specify whether it's for bread (high protein), as opposed to all-purpose (usually lower in protein). Both will work well in our recipes. Most readily available whole wheat flour is all-purpose. Whole wheat pastry flour (also sometimes known as graham flour) is very low in protein but works fine when mixed with white flour. It's too low in protein to be used in 100 percent whole wheat, however.

Rye flour: Specialty catalogs offer a bewildering variety of rye flours. By our survey, it appears that one can get medium or dark rye flours, plus the very coarsely ground rye meal (sometimes labeled as pumpernickel or whole grain rye flour, depending on how coarsely it is ground). The flours have varying percentages of rye bran, but the labeling generally doesn't make this clear. Be aware, though, that the very coarse-ground, high-bran products will produce a coarser, denser loaf. Luckily, you will not be able to get overly persnickety about this ingredient, because in U.S. supermarkets, choices are usually limited to the high-bran, high-protein varieties. Typical choices include Hodgson Mill Stone-ground Whole Grain Rye and Bob's Red Mill Organic Stone-ground Dark Rye Flour. True "medium" rye, with reduced bran and protein, is available from King Arthur Flour (www.kingarthurflour.com/shop/) and it produces a rye loaf that's closer to commercial rye bread.

Semolina flour: Semolina is a major component of some Italian breads, where it lends a beautiful yellow color and spectacular flavor. The best semolina for bread is the finely ground "durum flour." It is available from Bob's Red Mill (often in groceries), or online or from mail-order sources such as King Arthur Flour (www.kingarthurflour.com/shop/).

Oats: We use rolled oats or oat flour in several recipes. It adds a wonderful hearty flavor and contributes to a toothsome texture, but it doesn't have any gluten content. So, like rye flour, it needs to be paired with all-purpose flour to produce a loaf that rises. Oat varieties sold as "old-fashioned" (indicating that they are not pre-cooked) are best.

Organic flours: We have to admit, we can't tell the difference from the standpoint of flavor or texture. If you like organic products, by all means use them (we often do). But they're not required, and they certainly cost more. One reason some people take up the bread-baking hobby is to be able to eat organic bread every day, as it is usually unavailable commercially or is prohibitively expensive. There are now a number of organic flour brands available in the supermarket, but the best selection remains at your local organic food co-op.

Water

We can't detect important differences between water sources. The flavors of wheat and yeast overwhelm the contribution of water to bread's flavor. We use ordinary tap water running through a home water filter, but that's only because it's what we drink at home. Assuming your own tap water tastes good enough to drink, use it filtered or unfiltered; we can't tell the difference in finished bread.

∽

Modern Yeast

It almost never fails if used before its expiration date, so you do not need to wait until the yeast "proofs" (bubbles), nor do you need to add sugar. We avoid proofing yeast because it consumes five precious minutes! But it's probably a good idea to add the yeast to the water as the very first added ingredient. This hydrates the yeast and ensures that you won't get undissolved granules in the dough.

Though the truth is that you don't have to wait for it to dissolve fully: Some modern recipes have you mix all the dry ingredients (including yeast) together before adding liquids, and they work fine. The same is true for the salt.

Yeast

Here's another area where obsessing about an ingredient can take all the fun out of baking. Use whatever yeast is readily available; with our approach you just won't be able to tell the difference between the various national brands of yeast, nor between instant, regular, granulated, or cake yeast (though you will have to double the quantity if you use cake yeast). The long storage time of our doughs seems to act as an equalizer between all of these. One strong recommendation, though: buy in bulk or in commercially available jars, rather than in envelopes. The envelopes end up being much more expensive if you do lots of bread baking. Between the two of us, we've had only one yeast failure in many years of baking, and it was with an outdated envelope. Excellent results can be had with bulk-purchased yeast. Just be sure it is fresh. *The real key to avoiding yeast failures is to use water that is no warmer than lukewarm, around 100°F. (Even cold water will work, though it will take longer). Hot water kills yeast.* After several days of high-moisture storage, yeasted dough begins to take on a flavor and aroma that approximates the natural sourdough starters used in many artisan breads. Sours and starters like *biga* (Italian), *levain* (French), and *poolish* (referred to in Italian, French, and eastern European recipes) all require significant time and attention.

Salt

Food professionals agree that "artisan" salt, with its aromatic flavorings, tastes exactly like non-iodized table salt in cooked foods. Neither of us is able to distinguish among salt types in baked breads. Our recipes were tested with non-iodized *coarse* salt (such as kosher salt). If you use a finer salt (like table salt), decrease the salt volume by one-quarter (use only three-quarters as much salt), since it compacts more tightly than coarse salt.

Seeds, Nuts, and Chocolate

Caraway seeds: These are so central to the flavor of many rye breads that a lot of people think that caraway is actually the flavor of the rye grain. It's not, but for us, something does seem to be missing in unseeded rye bread. The only problem you can run into with caraway seeds (or any other) is that in very old ones the internal oil may have gone rancid. Taste a few if your jar is older than a year. Otherwise use whatever brand or bulk source you like.

Other seeds: Poppy, sesame, and pumpkin seeds are featured in a number of our recipes. They occasionally turn rancid, so taste a few if your jar is older than a year.

Nuts: Store in the freezer so the oils will not go rancid. Buy them either natural or blanched.

Chocolate: Some of our enriched breads call for chocolate, either cocoa powder, bar chocolate, or chunks. You will notice an improvement in flavor and recipe performance if you use the highest-quality chocolate available because of the purity of the ingredients. For bittersweet bar chocolate, Valrhona is our favorite, but Callebaut, Scharffen Berger, Lindt, Perugina, Ghirardelli, and other premium brands also work quite well. Our favorite unsweetened cocoa powder is Valrhona, but Droste's, Ghirardelli, and other premium brands also give good results. In our recipes, it doesn't matter if the cocoa powder is Dutch-processed (alkali-treated) or not: The question of Dutch-process is only important for baked goods risen with baking soda or baking powder. Yeast doesn't seem to care. If premium chocolates are unavailable, try the recipes with your favorite supermarket brands. The premium stuff is not an absolute requirement by any means.

3

EQUIPMENT

∽

More encyclopedic books will tell you everything you've ever wanted to know about an endless list of esoteric baker's accessories. In the spirit of our approach, we've tried to keep our list spare, and presented it in order of importance.

Oven thermometer: This is one item that isn't optional; you need it to calibrate your oven to get predictable bread-baking results. A hot oven drives excess water out of wet dough, but if it's too high you'll burn the crust before fully baking the crumb (the bread's interior). Home ovens are often off by up to 75 degrees. With an inexpensive oven thermometer, you can be certain to get results as good as ours are. Without the thermometer, your bread-baking experiments are going to require an annoying element of trial and error.

Baking stone: For best results, you'll want a high-quality, half-inch-thick baking stone (thin ones may crack within a year if used frequently). Look for a large one, preferably with a lifetime replacement guarantee against cracking (at the time of this book's writing, Williams-Sonoma was offering that warranty). The porous stone absorbs excess moisture from your wet dough, allowing a thin, crackling, crisp crust to form; this crust is one of the key elements in artisanal baking. Free-form loaves are baked right on the stone; liberal use of cornmeal or flour prevents sticking. You can bake wet dough on a cookie sheet or other non-porous surface, but the crust won't be as good.

A bucket or large plastic storage container with a lid: You can mix and store the dough in the same vessel and save yourself from having to wash one more item (it all figures into the five minutes a day). You need something large—a food-grade container that holds about five quarts. If you double the quantities in our recipes (resulting in a little less than eight pounds of dough), you'll need something on the order of nine or ten quarts. Great options are available from Tupperware, King Arthur Flour's Web site, and kitchen supply specialty stores. Less expensive plastic food containers are available from your local department store.

Broiler tray to hold boiling water for steam: This is essential for breads intended to achieve a crackling crust and nice caramelization. Most enriched breads (e.g., challah, brioche, et cetera) won't benefit from it, since the fat in their dough prevents the crackling crust.

Pizza peel: This is a flat board with a long handle used to slide bread and pizzas onto a hot stone. Wood or metal work equally well (you can't use anything made of plastic to transfer into the oven because of the contact with a very hot baking stone). Coat liberally with cornmeal before putting wet dough loaves on them or they will stick to the peel and/or the stone. If you don't have a pizza peel, a flat cookie sheet with no sides will do, but it will be more difficult to handle, as will a wood cutting board.

Cookie sheets and silicone mats: You may opt to bake your first bread on the cookie sheet that you already have in the house. Similar results are obtained with the new nonstick, flexible silicone baking mats, which don't need to be greased and are used on top of a cookie sheet (cleanup is a breeze). Or, you can line your cookie sheet with parchment paper, which also provides a nice non-stick surface and easy cleanup. All these nonporous options give respectable results, but don't expect a crackling crust.

Loaf pans: Like cookie sheets and silicone mats, loaf pans work well but don't promote the development of a great crackling crust. One word of caution about loaf pans: You *must* use a pan with a nonstick coating, and even then we find that a light greasing is needed. Our wet doughs will stick to traditional loaf pans no matter how much you grease and/or flour them. Nonstick loaf pans with the approximate dimensions of $9 \times 4 \times 3$ inches work best. Fill the pan a little more than half full.

Brioche pans: Traditionally, brioche is baked either in a fluted brioche mold or in a loaf pan. The fluted mold is easy to find either online or in any baking supply store. They are available in several sizes, with or without a nonstick coating; and flexible silicone brioche molds are now available.

Panettone molds: Large ceramic ramekins or ordinary fluted brioche pans work nicely, or you can buy an authentic panettone pan, or panettone molds made from paper.

Bread knife: A serrated bread knife is very helpful, because it does a great job cutting through fresh bread without tearing or compressing, and also because it's the best implement we've found for slashing high-moisture loaves just before baking the bread. Razor blades and French *lames* usually referenced in traditional artisan baking methods catch and stick in very wet dough; not so for serrated bread knives.

Cooling rack: These are the wire racks usually intended for cake. They are very helpful in preventing the soggy bottom crust that can result when you cool bread on a plate or other nonporous surface.

Dough scraper: Once you start making pizza and other rolled-out flat breads, you may want a rigid steel scraper to detach the dough when it sticks to your work surface. The dough scraper (sometimes referred to as a bench knife) is very useful for cutting wet dough into equal portions prior to making "ropes" for braided loaves. It's also the only easy way to scrape excess flour and cornmeal off your hot stone.

Measuring cups: There's only one word of advice: Avoid 2-cup measuring cups, because they overestimate the flour quantity when using the scoop-and-sweep method specified in our recipes.

Measuring spoons: Seek out a set that includes a half-tablespoon measure in addition to the usual suspects. Many of our recipes call for one and one-half tablespoons of salt and yeast. If you can't find a half-tablespoon measure, just measure out 1½ teaspoons.

Mixers and food processors. These are even easier than hand-mixing: If you're using a machine to mix dough, incorporating the flour is a snap. Whether you use a machine or mix by hand, your goal is to uniformly moisten all the flour and get rid of any dry patches (you can stop at that point). It will remain sticky but should hold a free-form loaf shape when you try to form one later in the recipe. With food processors, you'll need to add the dry ingredients first, then pour in the liquids, or there'll be some leakage around the bottom.

Pastry brushes: These look like small paintbrushes, and are used to paint cornstarch wash, egg wash, or water onto the surface of loaves just before baking.

Scales: We specify loaf size in pounds, but weighing is by no means necessary. We give both a weight and a visual cue for loaf size. A pound of dough is about the size of a grapefruit.

4

TIPS AND TECHNIQUES

This chapter will help you perfect your stored-dough, high-moisture breads. In the discussion that follows, we provide tips and techniques to achieve breads with a professional-quality crust (exterior) and crumb (interior).

Dough Moisture Content

Our recipes were carefully tested, and we arrived at the ratio of wet to dry ingredients with an eye toward creating a relatively "slack" and wet dough. But flours can vary in their protein content, the degree to which they're compacted into their containers, and in the amount of water they've absorbed from the environment. And environment changes; in most places, humidity will fluctuate over the course of the year. All of this means that the specified dry ingredients may produce slightly variable results depending on humidity, compaction, and the flour brand you're using.

If you're finding that the doughs are too stiff (especially if they don't show much rising capacity after a few days in the refrigerator), when making the next batches decrease the flour by a quarter cup at a time. And if they're too loose and wet, and don't hold a shape well for free-form loaves, increase the flour, again by a quarter cup at a time. You'll find that your overly wet dough still works better in loaf pans, where it can't spread sideways. The same is true for long-saved dough (more than 10 days or so).

Vary our recipes based on your taste. To summarize:

If you modify a recipe, using . . .	
. . . more liquid (giving you wetter dough), you'll get . . .	**. . . less liquid (giving you drier dough), you'll get . . .**
Larger air holes	Smaller air holes
Desirable "custard" interior (page 19), can become gummy if too little flour is used or too much whole grain is included	Difficult to achieve custard interior; interior will be drier
May be difficult for free-form loaf to hold shape, may spread laterally, but will do very well in loaf pans	Free-form loaves will hold shape well and remain high and domed
Requires less resting time before baking	Requires more resting time before baking

Storing Dough

In order to realize the ultimate value of our approach, and have daily artisan fresh-baked bread in only 5 minutes a day, you'll want to make enough dough to last a week or more. Your initial time investment (mixing the dough) is the most significant one, though it generally takes no more than 15 minutes. By mixing larger batches, you can spread that investment over more days of bread-making. So we really recommend mixing enough dough to last 7 to 10 days. For larger households, that might mean doubling, or even tripling the recipes as written in the book. Store the whole thing in a covered plastic container large enough to mix all the dough you need and accommodate the dough's rising.

"Custard" Crumb

Perfectly baked high-moisture dough can produce a delightful "custard" crumb (interior). Wheat flour's protein is gluten, and as the gluten cooks with water, it traps some of the water, creating a chewy and moist crumb, with a shiny and moist surface seen in the larger air holes. As you adjust flour amounts for your favorite recipes, you'll find that this is an effect you can manipulate. Too much flour, and you will lose the "custard" crumb character. Too little, and the dough will be difficult to shape and the breads gummy; this is easy to adjust. If your batch is too wet, you can work in more flour at the gluten-cloaking step, or in its storage container. If too dry, add more water, using wet hands at the shaping step.

Resting and Baking Times

All of our resting and baking times are approximate. Since loaves are formed by hand, their size will vary from loaf to loaf. There can be significant changes in resting and baking time requirements with changes in loaf size. Although large, flat loaves will bake rapidly, large, high-domed loaves will require dramatically longer baking times. So unless you're weighing out exact 1-pound loaves and forming the same shapes each time, your resting and baking times will vary and our listed time should be seen only as a starting point for 1-pound free-form loaves (1½-pound loaf-pan loaves). Here are some basic guidelines for varying resting and baking times and oven temperatures based on the characteristics of that day's loaf:

Increase resting and baking time if any of the following apply:

- Larger loaf
- More whole grain
- Wetter dough

Adjust baking temperature based on dough ingredients:

- Non-enriched doughs made mostly from white flour: 450°F
- Egg, honey, or brioche dough: 350°F
- High whole wheat content (more than 50 percent by volume): 350°F

Varying the Grain That Covers the Pizza Peel

After a short rest, most of our breads are slid off a pizza peel directly onto a hot baking stone. Cornmeal is the usual "lubricant" covering the peel and helping to slip the loaf off the peel and onto the stone. It prevents the loaf from sticking to either the pizza peel or the hot stone. But cornmeal is only one of many options. We tend to use cornmeal for the more rustic, full-flavored loaves, and whole wheat flour for the more delicate breads, like the French baguette. Even white flour works for the same purpose in pita and *ciabatta*. But coarser grains like cornmeal are the most "slippery," and fine-ground wheat flours may require a heavier coating to prevent sticking (sometimes you'll have to nudge the loaves off with a spatula or steel scraper). Mostly though, the choice of grain on the pizza peel is a matter of taste. We've used Malt-O-Meal cereal or oatmeal in a pinch, and Zoë's mom once used grits!

Underbaking Problems

Crust is hard and crispy when it emerges from the oven, but it softens as it comes to room temperature: This is most often a problem with very large breads, but it can happen with any loaf. The problem is that you've slightly underbaked the bread. The internal moisture, so high in wet dough, redistributes to the crust as the bread cools. If you haven't driven off enough water with heat, moisture will move from the interior (crumb) to the exterior (crust) and make it soft. As you gain experience, you will come to understand just how brown the loaf must be to prevent this problem with any given loaf size. We use brownness and crust firmness as our measure of doneness (there will be a few blackened bits on the loaf in non-egg breads). **If you have a crust that is initially crisp but softens as it cools, the bread can even be returned to the oven until you achieve the desired result.**

Loaf has a soggy or gummy crumb (interior): If it's really soggy, you have an underbaking problem.

- Check your oven temperature with a thermometer.
- Make sure you are allowing the dough to rest for the full time period we've recommended.
- Your dough may benefit from being a little drier. For the next batch, increase the flour by a quarter cup (or decrease the liquids a little) and check the result.
- If you're baking a large loaf (more than 1 pound), let it rest longer, and let it bake longer by 10 to 15 minutes.

One final word of advice: if you're finding the breads just a little gummy, **don't slice or eat your loaves when they're still warm.** We know, hot bread has a certain romance, so it's hard to wait for it to cool. But waiting will improve the texture, and when cool, the loaves don't compress so easily when cut. A sharp bread knife will go right through cooled crust and crumb with minimal compression.

Top crust won't crisp and brown nicely:

- Be sure you're using a baking stone where called for, and preheat it for at least 20 minutes, in an oven whose temperature has been checked with a thermometer.
- Bake with steam when called for, and be sure to close the oven door quickly after pouring hot water onto the steam tray to trap steam, which is key to creating a crackling crust.

If you're a crisp crust fanatic, we'll give you one ultimate approach to baking the perfect crust, but it takes some extra work (this does not apply to enriched breads). Start the loaf on the bottom shelf, directly on the stone. Two-thirds of the way through baking, transfer the loaf from the stone on the bottom shelf directly to a rack on the top shelf of the oven, removing the water pan (leave the stone where it is). Top crusts brown best near the top of the oven, and bottom crusts brown best near the bottom. This approach is particularly helpful with hard-crusted loaf-pan breads, where popping the bread out of the pan and transferring shelves makes a big difference in the crispness of the side and bottom crusts.

With this approach, you can permanently park your baking stone on the very lowest rack, where it will help even out the heat for everything you bake, not just bread. Then there'll be no need to shift around the stone or racks just because you're baking bread.

Overbaking Problems

The crust is great, but the crumb (interior) is dry:

- The bread may be overbaked. Again, make sure your oven is calibrated properly, using an oven thermometer.
- Another possibility is that the dough was dry to begin with. In traditional recipes, there's usually an instruction that reads something like "knead thoroughly, until the mass of dough is smooth, elastic, and less sticky, adding flour as needed." This often means too much flour gets added. Be careful not to add much additional flour when shaping.

Flour blobs in the middle of the slices: These are usually related to having added too much flour. Using wet hands to incorporate the last bits of flour will take care of this problem.

Shaping Problems

Loaf flattens and spreads sideways while resting on the pizza peel: If every loaf is ending up as flat bread, there are several possible explanations.

- The dough is *too* wet: This is often the problem when mixing by hand and there's an incentive to cut off the flour too soon (it's easier on your wrists).
- Not enough flour was dusted onto the dough while shaping and cloaking the loaf.

- The dough is too old: At about the point where it becomes "weepy," with liquid separating out from the dough, it's probably lost too much rising power to produce beautiful, domed loaves. It will still taste good, but it will turn into flat bread every time, unless you bake it in a loaf pan.

Odd-shaped loaves: If you haven't used enough cornmeal or flour on the pizza peel, a spot of dough may stick to it. As you slide the loaf off the peel, the spot pulls, causing an odd-shaped loaf. Solution: Use more cornmeal or flour on the pizza peel, especially if the dough is particularly sticky. You may also add flour to the dough during the cloaking and shaping step.

Other causes of odd-shaped loaves include not slashing deeply enough, and not letting the shaped loaves rest long enough before baking.

Storing Bread

Bread is at its best when it has completely cooled after baking. Hot or warm bread has a romantic appeal, but it cuts poorly and dries out quickly. And that certainly doesn't make for good storing characteristics. Having said that, sometimes we just can't resist!

We've found that the best way to keep bread fresh once it has been cut is to store it cut side down on a flat, nonporous surface like a plate or a clean countertop. Don't use foil, plastic wrap, or bags, which trap humidity. This softens the crust by allowing it to absorb water. An exception is pita bread, which is supposed to have a soft crust and can be stored in a plastic bag once cooled.

Breads made with whole grains or lots of water, and breads made with dough that has been well aged stay fresh longest. Keep that in mind if you would prefer to bake every other day. Use day-old bread for making bread crumbs in the food processor, or try one of our recipes like *panzanella* (page 48), bread puddings (pages 234 and 237), or *fattoush* (page 166). Or recycle your stale bread into new loaves as *"altus"* (page 67).

Parbaking Artisan Breads

Parbaking means partially baking your loaves, with the intention of finishing the baking later. In our attempt to improve the quality of our lives and the food we eat while reducing the time spent doing just that, we decided to test the concept of parbaking. Parbaking allows you to do all the shaping and most of the baking at home, and then complete it later. The parbaked bread can even be frozen. The perfect opportunity for this approach is when you're invited to a friends' house for dinner. Complete the baking in their oven and you present an absolutely fresh and warm bread for the dinner party.

Baking instructions for parbaked bread:

1. Follow preparation steps for any recipe in this book.

2. Begin baking at the recipe's usual temperature.

3. Remove the loaf from the oven when it just begins to darken in color; the idea is to set the center of the loaf. For most loaves, that means about 90 percent of the baking time.

4. Allow the loaf to cool on a rack, and then place in a plastic bag. Freeze immediately if you plan on storing bread for more than a day. If you don't have time to let the loaf cool, transport it in a brown paper bag to allow moisture to escape or the bread may become soggy.

To complete the baking:

1. If frozen, completely defrost the loaf at room temperature. Place on a baking stone in an oven preheated to the recipe's recommended temperature. Bake until browned and appealing, usually about 5 to 10 minutes.

2. Cool on a rack as usual.

5

THE MASTER RECIPE

∾

W e chose the artisan free-form loaf called the French boule as the basic model for all the breads in this book. The dough is made with
white flour, yeast, salt, and water; it is the easiest to handle and most
reliable to bake successfully. The white dough is used to make all the recipes in
Chapter 5; later chapters and recipes introduce other flours and flavors. The
round free-form shape of the boule *("boule"* in French means "ball") is the easiest to master. You'll learn how wet the dough needs to be (wet, but not so wet
that the finished loaf won't hold its shape) and how a "gluten cloak" substitutes
for kneading. And you'll learn a truly revolutionary approach to bread baking:
Take the needed amount of pre-mixed dough from the refrigerator, shape it,
leave it to rest, then pop it in the oven and let it bake while you're preparing the
rest of the meal.

Keep your dough wet—wetter doughs create an environment that favors
the development of sourdough character over the week of storage. And by omit-
ting kneading, by mixing dough in bulk, then storing and using it as it's needed
over time, you'll truly be able to make this bread in 5 minutes a day (excluding
resting and oven time). **You should become familiar with the following recipe
before going through the rest of the book.**

The Master Recipe: Boule (Artisan Free-Form Loaf)

Makes four 1-pound loaves. The recipe is easily doubled or halved.

3 cups lukewarm water
1½ tablespoons granulated yeast (1½ packets)
1½ tablespoons kosher or other coarse salt
6½ cups unsifted, unbleached, all-purpose white flour, measured with the
    scoop-and-sweep method
Cornmeal for pizza peel

Mixing and Storing the Dough

1. **Warm the water slightly:** It should feel just a little warmer than body
    temperature, about 100°F. Warm water will rise the dough to the right
    point for storage in about 2 hours. You can use cold tap water and get
    an identical final result; then the first rising will take 3 or even 4
    hours. That won't be too great a difference, as you will only be doing
    this once per stored batch.π

2. **Add yeast and salt to the water** in a 5-quart bowl or, preferably, in a
    resealable, lidded (not airtight) plastic food container or food-grade
    bucket. Don't worry about getting it all to dissolve.

3. **Mix in the flour—kneading is unnecessary:** Add all of the flour at
    once, measuring it in with dry-ingredient measuring cups, by gently
    scooping up flour, then sweeping the top level with a knife or spatula;
    don't press down into the flour as you scoop or you'll throw off the
    measurement by compressing. Mix with a wooden spoon, a high-
    capacity food processor (14 cups or larger) fitted with the dough
    attachment, or a heavy-duty stand mixer fitted with the dough hook
    until the mixture is uniform. If you're hand-mixing and it becomes
    too difficult to incorporate all the flour with the spoon, you can reach

into your mixing vessel with very wet hands and press the mixture together. Don't knead! It isn't necessary. You're finished when everything is uniformly moist, without dry patches. This step is done in a matter of minutes, and will yield a dough that is wet and loose enough to conform to the shape of its container.

4. **Allow to rise:** Cover with a lid (not airtight) that fits well to the container you're using. Do not use screw-topped bottles or Mason jars, which could explode from the trapped gases. Lidded plastic buckets designed for dough storage are readily available (page 14). Allow the mixture to rise at room temperature until it begins to collapse (or at least flattens on the top), approximately 2 hours, depending on the room's temperature and the initial water temperature. Longer rising times, up to about 5 hours, will not harm the result. You can use a portion of the dough any time after this period. Fully refrigerated wet dough is less sticky and is easier to work with than dough at room temperature. So, the first time you try our method, it's best to refrigerate the dough overnight (or at least 3 hours), before shaping a loaf.

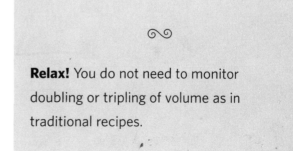

The scoop-and-sweep method gives consistent results without sifting or weighing. It's easier to scoop and sweep if you store your flour in a bin rather than the bag it's sold in; it can be hard to get the measuring cups in a bag without making a mess. Also: **Don't use an extra-large 2-cup-capacity measuring cup,** which allows the flour to overpack and measures too much flour.

Relax! You do not need to monitor doubling or tripling of volume as in traditional recipes.

On Baking Day

5. **The gluten cloak: *don't* knead, just "cloak" and shape a loaf in 30 to 60 seconds.** First, prepare a pizza peel by sprinkling it liberally with cornmeal (or whatever your recipe calls for) to prevent your loaf from sticking to it when you slide it into the oven.

   Sprinkle the surface of your refrigerated dough with flour. Pull up and cut off a 1-pound (grapefruit-size) piece of dough, using a serrated knife. Hold the mass of dough in your hands and add a little more flour as needed so it won't stick to your hands. Gently stretch the surface of the dough around to the bottom on all four sides, rotating the ball a quarter-turn as you go. Most of the dusting flour will fall off; it's not intended to be incorporated into the dough. The bottom of the loaf may appear to be a collection of bunched ends, but it will flatten out and adhere during resting and baking. The correctly shaped final product will be smooth and cohesive. The entire process should take no more than 30 to 60 seconds.

6. **Rest the loaf and let it rise on a pizza peel:** Place the shaped ball on the cornmeal-covered pizza peel. Allow the loaf to rest on the peel for about 40 minutes (it doesn't need to be covered during the rest period). Depending on the age of the dough, you may not see much rise during this period; more rising will occur during baking ("oven spring").

7. **Twenty minutes before baking, preheat the oven to 450°F,** with a baking stone placed on the middle rack. Place an empty broiler tray for holding water on any other shelf that won't interfere with the rising bread.

8. **Dust and slash:** Unless otherwise indicated in a specific recipe, dust the top of the loaf liberally with flour, which will allow the slashing knife to pass without sticking. Slash a ¼-inch-deep cross, "scallop," or tic-tac-toe pattern into the top, using a serrated bread knife (see photo below).

❧

What's a "gluten-cloak"? Just imagine a warm blanket being pulled around you on a cold night. Or, for the more technically inclined: What you are trying to do here is to add enough flour to the surface so it can be handled and the protein strands in the surface can be aligned, creating a resilient "cloak" around the mass of wet, barely kneaded dough. Visualize a cloak being pulled around the dough, so that the entire ball is surrounded by a skin. *Resist the temptation* to get rid of all stickiness by adding too much flour. Adding large amounts of flour prevents the bread from achieving a finished crumb with the typical artisanal "custard" (page 19).

9. **Baking with steam:** After a 20-minute preheat, you're ready to bake, even though your oven thermometer won't yet be up to full temperature. With a quick forward jerking motion of the wrist, slide the loaf off the pizza peel and onto the preheated baking stone. Quickly but carefully pour about 1 cup of hot water from the tap into the broiler tray and close the oven door to trap the steam. Bake for about 30 minutes, or until the crust is nicely browned and firm to the touch. Because you've used wet dough, there is little risk of drying out the interior, despite the dark crust. When you remove the loaf from the oven, it will audibly crackle, or "sing," when initially exposed to room-temperature air. Allow to cool completely, preferably on a wire cooling rack, for best flavor, texture, and slicing. The perfect crust may initially soften, but will firm up again when cooled.

10. **Store the remaining dough in the refrigerator in your lidded (not airtight) container and use it over the next 14 days:** You'll find that even one day's storage

improves the flavor and texture of your bread. This maturation continues over the 14-day storage period. Refrigerate unused dough in a lidded storage container (again, not airtight). If you mixed your dough in this container, you've avoided some cleanup. Cut off and shape more loaves as you need them. We often have several types of dough storing in the refrigerator at once. The dough can also be frozen in 1-pound portions in an airtight container and defrosted overnight in the refrigerator prior to baking day.

VARIATION: HERB BREAD. This simple recipe shows off the versatility of our approach. Herb-scented breads are great favorites for appetizers and snacks.

Follow the directions for mixing the Boule dough and add 1 teaspoon dried thyme leaves (2 teaspoons fresh) and ½ teaspoon dried rosemary leaves (1 teaspoon fresh) to the water mixture.

You can also use herbs with the other bread recipes in this chapter.

∽

Lazy sourdough shortcut: When your dough bucket is finally empty, don't wash it! Immediately re-mix another batch in the same container. In addition to saving the cleanup step, the aged dough stuck to the sides of the container will give your new batch a head start on sourdough flavor. Just scrape it down and it will hydrate and incorporate into the new dough.

∽

Amaze your friends with the "6-3-3-13" rule: If you want to store enough for eight one-pound loaves, here's a simple mnemonic for the recipe: 6, 3, 3, and 13. It's 6 cups water, 3 tablespoons salt, 3 tablespoons yeast, and then add 13 cups of flour. Store in a 10-quart lidded container. That's it. It will amaze your friends when you do this in their homes without a recipe—but tell them to buy this book anyway!

Baguette

This is the quintessential thin and crusty loaf of France, served at every meal, and the symbol of their entire cuisine. We both traveled there with our spouses, years apart, and had the same response to the mood, to the light, to the sounds, and maybe most of all, to the flavors, especially the baguettes.

A twenty-minute rest after shaping is all that is needed to create a light and airy loaf. So our baguette is delicious, and very, very fast.

"On my honeymoon in France we survived on $25 a day, and this included accommodations. Every morning we would go to the café for a baguette and café au lait. For lunch it was a tartine (page 34), and dinner was often the same with the addition of the bottle of wine and pastry to follow. We didn't eat lavishly, but we ate well. The baguettes were essential. It's hard to match this experience in the States, but we've found we can come very close with this recipe."—Zoë

Baguettes are defined as much by their crust as their crumb (the bread's interior). The crust dominates the mouth sensation. Aside from the shape, one important technique that differentiates the baguette from the boule in this chapter is that the baguette is *not* heavily dusted with flour, at least not traditionally. So, to keep the knife from sticking, brush water onto the surface of the loaf just before slashing. You'll also notice that this loaf uses whole wheat flour rather than cornmeal on the pizza peel, since cornmeal would impart too strong a flavor for classic baguettes. Traditional recipes for baguettes are high maintenance, so if you've done this the old-fashioned way, our approach should be a relief. With your fresh baguette, create a sensational meal by making an Aubergine Tartine (page 34).

Makes 1 large or 2 small baguettes

1 pound (grapefruit-size portion) Boule dough (page 26)
Whole wheat flour for the pizza peel

1. **Preheat the oven to 450°F** with a baking stone placed on the middle rack. Place an empty broiler tray on any other shelf that won't interfere with the rising bread.

2. Dust the surface of the refrigerated dough with flour and cut off a 1-pound (grapefruit-size) piece. Dust the piece with more flour and shape it into a ball by stretching the surface of the dough around to the bottom on all four sides, rotating the ball a quarter-turn as you go. Once it's cohesive, begin to stretch and elongate the dough, dusting with additional flour as necessary. You may find it helpful to roll it back and forth with your hands on a flour-dusted surface. Form a cylinder approximately 2 inches in diameter. If the loaf won't fit on your pizza peel or stone, cut it in half to make two smaller baguettes. Place the loaf/loaves on a pizza peel covered with whole wheat flour and allow to rest for 20 minutes.

3. After the dough has rested, paint water over the surface of the loaf using a pastry brush. The water prevents the knife from sticking in the wet dough, and an authentic baguette isn't flour-dusted on the top crust. Slash the loaf with longitudinal cuts that move diagonally across the loaf, using a serrated bread knife.

4. Slide the loaf directly onto the hot stone. Pour 1 cup of hot tap water into the broiler tray, and quickly close the oven door. Bake for about 25 minutes, or until deeply browned and firm to the touch.

5. Allow to cool on a rack before cutting or eating.

Aubergine Tartine

This open-faced sandwich is a more sophisticated and vegetarian cousin to our Croque Monsieur (page 206), with smoky grilled eggplant *(aubergine)* and red pepper on freshly baked Baguette (page 32), topped with spicy greens and soft, ripe cheese.

Makes 1 open-faced baguette sandwich to serve 3 or 4

2 half-inch thick pieces of lengthwise-sliced eggplant
Olive oil for brushing eggplant
Salt and pepper to taste
½ red pepper
½ baguette (see page 32)
2 cloves roasted garlic (see page 118)
1 dozen arugula leaves
3 ounces soft ripened cheese such as Brie or Camembert, sliced

1. Preheat a gas or charcoal grill, or a broiler. Brush the eggplant slices with olive oil. Sprinkle with salt and pepper and grill over a medium gas flame or charcoal, or under a broiler, until browned and soft but not overcooked, approximately 5 minutes on each side.

2. Cut the pepper into quarters and then flatten the pieces, making additional cuts as needed to flatten. Grill or broil the pepper under the broiler or on the gas or charcoal grill, keeping the skin side closest to the heat source. Check often and remove when the skin is blackened, about 8 to 10 minutes. Drop the roasted pieces into an empty bowl and cover it. The skin will loosen over the next ten minutes. Gently hand-peel the pepper and discard the blackened skin. Some dark bits will adhere to the pepper's flesh, which won't be a problem. Cut the red pepper into thin ribbons.

3. Split the baguette lengthwise, spread it open, and tear out some of the inside. Smear roasted garlic (page 118) over the cut surface. Top with eggplant and sliced red pepper. Spread arugula over the pepper.

4. Top with the cheese and broil or grill for 3 to 4 minutes, until the cheese is melted, taking care not to burn the baguettes.

Bâtard

This short and wide baguette-style loaf is easier to use for sandwiches because there's more of the chewy interior compared to the crustier baguette. Accordingly, the flavor leans toward the mellow sweetness of the crumb rather than the crisp caramelization of the crust. Depending on your preference, this loaf can be almost as wide as a sandwich loaf, but typically it is about three inches across at its widest point. Like baguettes, the *bâtard* is tapered to a point at each end.

Makes 1 bâtard

1 pound (grapefruit-size portion) Boule dough (page 26)
Whole wheat flour for the pizza peel

1. Follow steps 1 and 2 for the baguette on page 32, but shape the loaf to a diameter of about 3 inches.

2. When rolling the loaf on the floured surface, concentrate pressure at the ends to form the *bâtard's* traditional taper.

3. Follow steps 3 through 5 for the baguette, but increase the baking time to 30 minutes, or until deeply brown.

Ciabatta

The word *ciabatta* is Italian for slipper, and refers to the shape of the bread, which is halfway between a flatbread and a loaf-shaped bread. It's made from very wet dough, shaped as a elongated oval or rectangle (perhaps you have slippers shaped like this?). To achieve the very moist crumb, shape the loaf with wet hands, rather than dusting with flour. The bread will be chewy and moist, with large and appealing air holes. *Ciabatta* is baked without cornmeal on the bottom, so dust the pizza peel with a thick coating of white flour instead. And, since white flour is a less efficient "stick-preventer" than cornmeal, you may need to nudge the loaf off the peel with a steel dough scraper or spatula.

Makes 1 ciabatta

1 pound (grapefruit-size portion) Boule dough (page 26)
White flour for the pizza peel

1. Cut off a 1-pound (grapefruit-size) piece of refrigerated dough without dusting the surface with flour; wet hands will help prevent sticking. Using your wet hands, shape the dough into a ball by stretching the surface of the dough around to the bottom on all four sides, rotating the ball a quarter-turn as you go. With your wet fingers, flatten the ball into an elongated oval about ¾ inch thick. Don't make it thinner than ¾ inch, or it will puff like pita bread, which isn't desirable here.

2. **Twenty minutes before baking time, preheat the oven to 450°F,** with a baking stone placed on the middle rack. Place an empty broiler tray on any other shelf that won't interfere with the rising bread.

3. Place the loaf on a flour-covered pizza peel and allow to rest for 20 minutes. Dust the top with flour, but don't slash the loaf.

4. Slide the loaf directly onto the hot stone. Pour 1 cup of hot tap water into the broiler tray, and quickly close the oven door. Bake for about 20 minutes, or until deeply brown.

5. Allow to cool on a rack before cutting or eating.

Couronne

This ring or crown-shaped French loaf is a specialty of Lyon. It's quite simple to shape and is a beautiful crustier alternative to the classic boule (see color photo insert).

Makes 1 couronne

1 pound (grapefruit-size portion) Boule dough (page 26)
Whole wheat flour for the pizza peel

1. Dust the surface of the flour and cut off a 1-pound (grapefruit-size) piece. Dust the piece with more flour and quickly shape it into a ball by stretching the surface of the dough around to the bottom on all four sides, rotating the ball a quarter-turn as you go. When a cohesive ball has formed, poke your thumbs through the center of the ball and gradually stretch the hole so that it will be large enough to stay open during the bread's oven-rise. This means that the hole will need to be about three times as wide as the wall of the ring.

2. Place the loaf on a pizza peel covered with whole wheat flour and allow to rest for 40 minutes.

3. **Twenty minutes before baking time, preheat the oven to 450°F**, with a baking stone placed on the middle rack. Place an empty broiler tray on any other shelf that won't interfere with the rising bread.

4. Just before baking, dust the *couronne* with flour and slash radially, like spokes in a wheel (see color photo insert).

5. Slide the loaf directly onto the hot stone. Pour 1 cup of hot tap water into the broiler tray, and quickly close the oven door. Bake for about 30 minutes, or until deeply browned and firm. Smaller or larger loaves will require adjustments in baking time.

6. Allow the bread to cool before cutting or eating.

Pain d'Epi (Wheat Stalk Bread)

This is a simple yet impressive bread to present to guests (see color photo insert). You may find that you get more well-defined "wheat grains" when you substitute high-protein bread flour for the all-purpose flour listed below. If you use all-purpose flour, increase it to 7 cups. The bread can also be made with our master white dough (see Boule, page 26), but the illusion of the wheat grains won't be quite so well-defined.

"I first ate pain d'epi *when vacationing in the south of France. Maman, our adopted grandmother and host, had it delivered fresh every morning. I'd walk through a yard filled with fruit and herb trees to a special bread basket that hung next to the mailbox. I'd pick up this freshly baked wheat stalk and have to pinch myself to make sure it wasn't a dream. The bread was impossibly light, crisp, and absolutely perfect with coffee and jam in the morning, or with Maman's fish stew for dinner. It was heaven!"—Zoë*

Makes four 1-pound loaves. The recipe is easily doubled or halved.

3 cups lukewarm water
1½ tablespoons granulated yeast (1½ packets)
1½ tablespoons salt
6½ cups bread flour (or substitute 7 cups all-purpose)
Whole wheat flour for the pizza peel

1. **Mixing and storing the dough:** Mix the yeast and salt with the water.

2. Mix in the flour without kneading, using a spoon, a 14-cup capacity food processor (with dough attachment), or a heavy-duty stand mixer (with dough hook). If you're not using a machine, you may need to use wet hands to get the last bit of flour to incorporate.

3. Cover (not airtight), and allow to rest at room temperature until the dough rises and collapses (or flattens on top); approximately 2 hours.

4. The dough can be used immediately after the initial rise, though it is easier to handle when cold. Refrigerate in a lidded (not airtight) container and use over the next 14 days.

5. **On baking day,** dust the surface of the refrigerated dough with flour and cut off a 1-pound (grapefruit-size) piece. Dust the piece with more flour and quickly shape it into a ball by stretching the surface of the dough around to the bottom on all four sides, rotating the ball a quarter-turn as you go. Gradually elongate the mass. With the palms of your hands, gently roll it into the shape of a baguette, tapering the ends to points.

6. Allow to rest and rise on a whole wheat–covered pizza peel for 30 minutes. Do not slash.

7. **Twenty minutes before baking time, preheat the oven to 450°F,** with a baking stone placed on the middle rack. Place an empty broiler tray on any other shelf that won't interfere with the rising bread. Just before

baking time, dust the loaf with flour. With a sharp pair of kitchen scissors, cut from the top, at a 45-degree angle into the dough, stopping a quarter-inch from the bottom. Fold each cut piece over to the side, alternating sides with each cut. Repeat until the entire loaf is cut and *pain d'epi* formed (see photo, opposite).

8. Slide the loaf directly onto the hot stone. Pour 1 cup of hot tap water into the broiler tray, and quickly close the oven door. Bake for about 25 minutes, or until the loaf is deeply browned and firm.

9. Allow to cool before breaking off the wheat-stalk shapes. Slather with butter and eat warm if you can't wait!

Crusty White Sandwich Loaf

This loaf is nothing like commercial white bread, that impossibly soft stuff best used for wadding up and tossing across lunchrooms. The crust is firm if not actually crackling. If you're looking for a flavorful, *soft-crusted*, and buttery loaf, closer to what most kids are used to, you'll probably want to try Soft American-Style White Bread (page 204) or Buttermilk Bread (page 207). The stored dough adds sourdough complexity to the traditionally bland product, and the steam adds both crackle and caramelization to the crust.

This variation will give you some experience baking high-moisture dough in a loaf pan. You *must* use a nonstick pan; they work well but still require a light greasing. Wet dough usually sticks miserably to traditional pans no matter how much you grease them.

Makes 1 loaf

1½ pounds (cantaloupe-size portion) Boule dough (page 26)
Neutral-tasting oil for greasing the pan

1. Dust the surface of the refrigerated dough with flour and cut off a 1½-pound (cantaloupe-size) piece. Dust with more flour and quickly shape it into a ball by stretching the surface of the dough around to the bottom on all four sides, rotating the ball a quarter-turn as you go. Lightly grease a 9×4×3-inch nonstick loaf pan with a neutral-flavored oil.

2. Elongate the ball into an oval and drop it into the prepared pan. You want to fill the pan slightly more than half full.

3. Allow the dough to rest for 1 hour and 40 minutes; (or just 40 minutes if you're using fresh, unrefrigerated dough). Dust with flour and slash the top crust with the tip of a serrated bread knife.

4. **Twenty minutes before baking time, preheat the oven to 450°F,** with an empty broiler tray on any other shelf that won't interfere with the rising bread. A baking stone is not essential when using a loaf pan; if you omit it, you can shorten the preheat to 5 minutes.

5. Place the loaf on a rack near the center of the oven. Pour 1 cup of hot tap water into the broiler tray and quickly close the oven door. Bake for about 35 minutes, or until brown and firm.

6. Remove the loaf from the pan and allow to cool completely on a rack before slicing or eating.

6

PEASANT LOAVES

The term "peasant bread" has come to mean the rougher, more rustic loaf that originated in the European countryside during the Middle Ages. These are breads made with whole-grain ingredients that, once upon a time, fell out of fashion with sophisticated European urbanites. How times have changed; since the 1980s, rustic breads now signal sophistication just as surely as a perfect French baguette. Forget sophistication; thank goodness we've come to realize the wonderful and complex flavors to be had by adding whole grains and rye to our bread.

Rye flour creates the tangy, slightly nutty fragrance and flavor that is basic to many of these breads, whether or not it's blended with whole wheat or other grains. Even if rye flour is not sold as "whole grain," it has more fiber (from rye bran) than white wheat flour. The proteins and starches in rye flour plus the extra boost of rye bran mean that the breads have a substantial texture and sensation when chewed.

European Peasant Bread

The round, whole-grain country-style loaves of rural France (*pain de campagne*) and Italy (*pane rustica*) were once the natural results of European poverty. White flour was once an almost unattainable luxury and the whole grains were reserved for the "help." Today people from all walks of life enjoy the crackling crust and moist chewy crumb that are the key sensations of this peasant bread.

We live in the upper Midwest, where in the wintertime we dream of vacations along the sunny Riviera. The next best thing to being there is mixing up a batch of this bread and serving it with anchovies, a strong cheese, and a hearty fish soup with lots of garlic and fresh herbs (see page 84). We are utterly transported!

Next day, cut up the the leftovers for Tuscan Bread Salad (page 48).

Makes four 1-pound loaves. The recipe is easily doubled or halved.

3 cups lukewarm water
1½ tablespoons granulated yeast (1½ packets)
1½ tablespoons salt
½ cup rye flour
½ cup whole wheat flour
5½ cups unbleached all-purpose flour
Cornmeal for the pizza peel

1. **Mixing and storing the dough:** Mix the yeast and salt with the water in a 5-quart bowl, or a lidded (not airtight) food container.

2. Mix in the remaining dry ingredients without kneading, using a spoon, a 14-cup capacity food processor (with dough attachment), or a heavy-duty stand mixer (with dough hook). If you're not using a machine, you may need to use wet hands to incorporate the last bit of flour.

3. Cover (not airtight), and allow to rest at room temperature until the dough rises and collapses (or flattens on top), approximately 2 hours.

4. The dough can be used immediately after the initial rise, though it is easier to handle when cold. Refrigerate in a lidded (not airtight) container and use over the next 14 days.

5. **On baking day**, dust the surface of the refrigerated dough with flour and cut off a 1-pound (grapefruit-size) piece. Dust with more flour and quickly shape it into a ball by stretching the surface of the dough around to the bottom on all four sides, rotating the ball a quarter-turn as you go. Allow to rest and rise on a cornmeal-covered pizza peel for 40 minutes.

6. **Twenty minutes before baking time, preheat the oven to 450°F,** with a baking stone placed on the middle rack. Place an empty broiler tray on any other shelf that won't interfere with the rising bread.

7. Sprinkle the loaf liberally with flour and slash a cross, "scallop," or tic-tac-toe pattern into the top, using a serrated bread knife (see photo, page 29). Leave the flour in place for baking; tap some of it off before slicing.

8. Slide the loaf directly onto the hot stone. Pour 1 cup of hot tap water into the broiler tray, and quickly close the oven door. Bake for about 35 minutes, or until the top crust is deeply browned and very firm. Smaller or larger loaves will require adjustments in baking time.

9. Allow to cool before slicing or eating.

Tuscan Bread Salad (Panzanella)

Even great bread goes stale; here's a delicious way to use it. European Peasant Bread is our first choice for *Panzanella*, but most other non-enriched, unsweetened breads will also work well. This salad is a masterpiece when made with tomatoes at the peak of the summer season. If you grow your own, here's your chance to let them shine. If you want to turn this into a complete vegetarian meal, add cooked or canned cannellini or Great Northern beans.

Makes 4 servings

The Salad
10 slices stale bread (1 to 3 days old), cubed
3 medium tomatoes, cubed
1 medium cucumber, sliced
1 very small red onion, thinly sliced
1 teaspoon capers
¼ cup pitted black olives, halved
2 anchovy fillets, chopped, optional
15 basil leaves, coarsely chopped
1 tablespoon coarsely grated Parmigiano-Reggiano cheese
¾ cup cooked or canned cannellini or Great Northern beans (optional)

The Dressing
⅓ cup extra-virgin olive oil
3 teaspoons red wine vinegar
1 garlic clove, finely minced
Salt and freshly ground pepper to taste (don't be stingy)

1. Prepare the salad ingredients and combine in a large salad bowl.

2. Whisk all the dressing ingredients until well blended.

3. Toss the dressing with the salad, and allow to stand for at least 10 minutes, or until the bread has softened.

Pan Bagna (Provençal Tuna and Vegetable Sandwich)

This sandwich loaf is a specialty of Provence, where generations of farm families came up with ways to use day-old country bread. *Pan bagna*, literally translated from the Provençal language, means "bathed bread." The sandwich is remarkably similar to a New Orleans muffuletta, which is based on cold cuts (usually ham, salami, and mortadella) rather than tuna steak. In New Orleans, they use a local concoction called "olive salad" rather than sliced olives, and you probably won't find arugula on a muffuletta.

You'll have an easier time with this recipe if you shape a slightly flattened boule, rather than a high-domed one.

Makes 4 sandwich wedges

1-pound loaf European Peasant Bread (page 46), or French Boule (page 26)
4 tablespoons olive oil
1 small garlic clove
1 tablespoon red wine vinegar
Salt and freshly ground pepper
¼ pound soft goat cheese
6 Mediterranean-style olives, pitted and sliced
1 cup arugula leaves, rinsed and well dried
6 ounces cooked fresh tuna steak, thinly sliced, or substitute canned tuna in a
  pinch
3 small tomatoes, thinly sliced
10 large basil leaves, shredded

1. Slice the bread in half horizontally and slightly hollow out the top and the bottom. Make fresh bread crumbs out of the discarded centers and keep for another use. Drizzle the cut surface of the halves with 1½ tablespoons of the oil.

2. In a blender combine the remaining 2½ tablespoons of oil with the garlic, vinegar, and salt to taste. Blend the dressing until smooth.

3. Spread the goat cheese in the bottom shell and top it with the olives, arugula, and salt and pepper to taste. Drizzle with one-third of the dressing, top with the tuna, salt and pepper to taste, and drizzle half the remaining dressing over the tuna. Top the tuna with the tomatoes, basil, and salt and pepper to taste. Drizzle with the remaining dressing, and add the top of the loaf.

4. Wrap the sandwich in plastic, place it on a plate, and cover it with another plate with approximately 1 to 2 pounds of weight on top. Refrigerate for 1 hour, or eat right away if you can't wait. The sandwich may be made up to 6 hours in advance and kept covered and chilled.

5. Allow to come partway back to room temperature, cut the *pan bagna* into 2-inch slices, and serve.

VARIATION:

Make a New Orleans muffuletta sandwich by substituting sliced ham, salami, and mortadella for the tuna steak, provolone for the goat cheese, and lettuce for the arugula and basil leaves. If you're anywhere near New Orleans, pick up the local product called "olive salad" and use it in place of the sliced olives.

Olive Bread

This bread is associated with the countries of the Mediterranean, especially Italy and France, where the olives are abundant and have incredible flavor. Use the best-quality olives you can find; the wetter Kalamata style work as well as the dry Niçoise-type, so it's your choice. The rich salty flavors of the olives make this a perfect accompaniment to cheeses, pasta tossed with fresh tomatoes, or our Tuscan White Bean Dip (page 53).

Makes 1 Olive Bread

Use any of these pre-mixed doughs: Boule (page 26), European Peasant (page 46), Olive Oil (page 134), Light Whole Wheat (page 74), or Italian Semolina (page 80)

1 pound (grapefruit-size portion) of any pre-mixed dough listed above

¼ cup high-quality olives, pitted and halved

Cornstarch wash (see sidebar)

1. Dust the surface of the refrigerated dough with flour and cut off a grapefruit-size piece. Using your hands and a rolling pin, flatten the dough to a thickness of ½ inch. Cover with the olives and roll up to seal inside the dough. Dust with more flour and quickly shape it into a ball by stretching the surface of the dough around to the bottom on all four sides, rotating the ball a quarter-turn as you go. Allow to rest and rise on a cornmeal-covered pizza peel for 1 hour.

Cornstarch Wash: Using a fork, blend ½ teaspoon cornstarch with a small amount of water to form a paste. Add ½ cup water and whisk with the fork. Microwave or boil until mixture appears glassy, about 30 to 60 seconds on high. It will keep in the refrigerator for two weeks; discard if it has an off smell.

2. **Twenty minutes before baking time, preheat the oven to 450°F,** with a baking stone placed on the middle rack. Place an empty broiler tray on any other shelf that won't interfere with the rising bread.

3. Just before baking, paint the surface of the loaf with cornstarch wash, then slash a cross, "scallop," or tic-tac-toe pattern into the top, using a serrated bread knife (see photo, page 29).

4. Slide the loaf directly onto the hot stone. Pour 1 cup of hot tap water into the broiler tray, and quickly close the oven door. Bake for about 35 minutes, or until the top crust is deeply browned and very firm.

5. Allow to cool on a rack before slicing or eating.

Tuscan White Bean Dip

All across Europe, meals are made up of beans mixed with other savory flavors such as garlic and basil and served with a variety of meats. We created this dip in the spirit of simplifying our lives and eating foods with rich, wonderful flavors. Simply puree beans with the aromatics and spread it over our Olive Bread (page 51) to make this delicious rustic hors d'oeuvre.

It's probably easier to find dried White Northern beans than the more authentic cannellini beans, so go with whatever you can find. And if you don't have time to roast the garlic, raw is fine, though it will have a much stronger kick. Canned roasted red peppers can be substituted, but the flavor is less intense.

Makes about 2 cups of dip

1 cup dried White Northern or cannellini beans (or one 16-ounce can, drained)
1 small red bell pepper
1 large clove roasted garlic (page 118)
2 tablespoons extra virgin olive oil
1 teaspoon salt
Freshly ground pepper to taste
10 fresh basil leaves

1. Pick over the dried beans for stones, dirt, and debris. Rinse, drain, and then cover with water and soak overnight. Bring to a simmer and cook for 2 to 3 hours, or until soft, adding water as needed to keep the beans covered. Drain, reserving about 2 cups of the cooking liquid (though you probably won't need all of it). If using canned beans, discard the canning liquid and use plain water later in the recipe.

2. Cut the pepper into quarters, remove the core and seeds, and then flatten the pieces, cutting additional slits as needed. Grill or broil the pepper under the broiler or on a gas or charcoal grill until the skin is

blackened, about 8 to 10 minutes. Drop the roasted pepper into a tightly covered bowl and allow the skin to loosen by "steaming" in its own heat and moisture for 10 minutes or longer. Gently hand-peel the pepper and discard the blackened skin. Some dark bits will adhere to the pepper's flesh.

3. Peel the roasted garlic (page 118) and place it in the food processor along with the cooked beans, olive oil, salt and pepper. Process until smooth, adding some of the reserved cooking liquid or water until a medium consistency is reached.

4. Add the basil and roasted pepper and pulse until coarsely chopped; taste and adjust seasonings as needed.

5. Refrigerate and serve with European Peasant Bread (page 46) or Baguettes (page 32).

Tapenade Bread

We enjoy tapenade, the delightful French spread made from olives, anchovies, and capers. This recipe was originally developed with a store-bought tapenade, but then we started making our own. It was easy and had a freshness that the commercial product couldn't match. But if you have a jar of great tapenade on hand, by all means use it. This bread is great with cheeses or grilled with tomato, basil, and garlic into mouth-watering Bruschetta (page 57).

Makes four 1-pound loaves. The recipe is easily doubled or halved.

The Tapenade (makes 1 to 2 cups)
½ pound pitted black olives
4 teaspoons capers, drained
4 anchovy fillets
1 garlic clove, put through a garlic press or very finely chopped
¼ teaspoon dried thyme
4 tablespoons olive oil

The Dough
3 cups lukewarm water
1½ tablespoons granulated yeast (1½ packets)
1 tablespoon salt
7 cups bread flour
1 cup homemade (above) or store-bought tapenade

1. **Making the tapenade:** Coarsely chop all the tapenade ingredients together in a food processor. Set aside.

2. **Mixing and storing the dough:** Mix the yeast and salt with the water in a 5-quart bowl, or a lidded (not airtight) food container.

3. Mix in the remaining ingredients without kneading, using a spoon, a 14-cup capacity food processor (with dough attachment), or a heavy-

duty stand mixer (with dough hook). If you're not using a machine, you may need to use wet hands to incorporate the last bit of flour.

4. Cover (not airtight), and allow to rest at room temperature until the dough rises and collapses (or flattens on top), approximately 2 hours.

5. The dough can be used immediately after the initial rise, though it is easier to handle when cold. Refrigerate in a lidded (not airtight) container and use over the next 7 days.

6. **On baking day,** dust the surface of the refrigerated dough with flour and cut off a 1-pound (grapefruit-size) piece. Dust the piece with more flour and quickly shape it into a ball by stretching the surface of the dough around to the bottom on all four sides, rotating the ball a quarter-turn as you go. Allow to rest and rise on a cornmeal-covered pizza peel for 1 hour.

7. **Twenty minutes before baking time, preheat the oven to 450°F,** with a baking stone placed on the middle rack. Place an empty broiler tray on any other shelf that won't interfere with the rising bread.

8. Sprinkle the loaf liberally with flour and slash a cross, "scallop," or tic-tac-toe pattern into the top, using a serrated bread knife (see photo, page 29). Leave the flour in place for baking; tap some of it off before eating.

9. Slide the loaf directly onto the hot stone. Pour 1 cup of hot tap water into the broiler tray, and quickly close the oven door. Bake 35 to 40 minutes, or until deeply browned and firm. Smaller or larger loaves will require adjustments in baking time.

10. Allow to cool before slicing or eating.

Bruschetta

Here's one more way to use stale bread, which, like *Panzanella* (page 48), also comes from Italy. The Italians continually rearrange and reconstruct a limited number of delicious ingredients: bread, tomato, garlic, olive oil, and herbs. Every family seems to have its own take on the combo.

"This was first made for me by my friend Marco, who was a visiting student from Livorno in Italy. He wanted to show off his family specialties, so he made a pasta dish with Parmigiano-Reggiano that he'd carried from Italy in his luggage, and to accompany it, this simple but memorable bruschetta."—Jeff

Makes 4 bruschetti appetizers

4 thick slices of day-old Tapenade Bread (page 55), French Boule (page 26),
   or other non-enriched bread
1 garlic clove, cut in half
¼ cup seeded and chopped tomato, well drained
8 torn or chopped fresh basil leaves
Coarse salt
4 teaspoons extra virgin olive oil

1. **Preheat the oven to 400°F.** Toast (or grill) the bread slices until nicely crisp and browned.

2. Rub the pieces on both sides with the cut flat sides of the garlic. This will actually grate the raw garlic down into the toasted bread. Rub as much or as little as you like.

3. Place the bruschetti on a cookie sheet and top with the tomato, basil, and a sprinkling of coarse salt. Finish with a liberal drizzling of olive oil; about a teaspoon per slice.

4. Bake for about 5 minutes, or until hot. Serve as an appetizer.

Deli-Style Rye

This loaf, our version of a classic sourdough rye, started Jeff's 20-year obsession with bread baking. This method produces a traditional rye comparable to those made with complicated starters—the kind that need to be "fed," incubated, and kept alive in your refrigerator. It makes a very nice loaf to eat on day one, but will be even better on day two or three. It is great with butter and it is perfect for our Reuben Sandwich (page 60).

Along with the caraway seeds, which give this bread its classic flavor, what sets this rye apart from other rustic breads is that there is no flour on the top crust; instead it's glazed with a cornstarch wash, which serves the triple function of anchoring the caraway seeds, allowing the slashing knife to pass easily without sticking, and giving the loaf a beautiful shine.

"My grandmother truly did believe that this rye loaf was better than cake. It turns out that elder immigrants from all over Europe felt the same way about 'a good piece of bread.' Friends of Dutch and Scandinavian heritage also recall older immigrant relatives shunning ordinary desserts in favor of extraordinary bread."—Jeff

Makes four 1-pound loaves. The recipe is easily doubled or halved.

3 cups lukewarm water
1½ tablespoons granulated yeast (1½ packets)
1½ tablespoons salt
1½ tablespoons caraway seeds, plus more for sprinkling on the top
1 cup rye flour
5½ cups unbleached all-purpose flour
Cornmeal for pizza peel
Cornstarch wash (see sidebar, page 51)

1. **Mixing and storing the dough:** Mix the yeast, salt, and caraway seeds with the water in a 5-quart bowl, or a lidded (not airtight) food container.

2. Mix in the remaining dry ingredients without kneading, using a spoon, a 14-cup capacity food processor (with dough attachment), or a heavy-duty stand mixer (with dough hook). If you're not using a machine, you may need to use wet hands to incorporate the last bit of flour.

3. Cover (not airtight), and allow to rest at room temperature until the dough rises and collapses (or flattens on top), approximately 2 hours.

4. The dough can be used immediately after the initial rise, though it is easier to handle when cold. Refrigerate in a lidded (not airtight) container and use over the next 14 days.

5. **On baking day,** dust the surface of the refrigerated dough with flour and cut off a 1-pound (grapefruit-size) piece. Dust the piece with more flour and quickly shape it into a ball by stretching the surface of the dough around to the bottom on all four sides, rotating the ball a quarter-turn as you go. Elongate the ball into an oval-shaped loaf. Allow to rest and rise on a cornmeal-covered pizza peel for 40 minutes.

6. **Twenty minutes before baking time, preheat the oven to 450°F,** with a baking stone placed on the middle rack. Place an empty broiler tray on any other shelf that won't interfere with the rising bread.

7. Using a pastry brush, paint the top crust with cornstarch wash and then sprinkle with additional caraway seeds. Slash with deep parallel cuts across the loaf, using a serrated bread knife.

8. Slide the loaf directly onto the hot stone. Pour 1 cup of hot tap water into the broiler tray, and quickly close the oven door. Bake for about 30 minutes, or until deeply browned and firm. Smaller or larger loaves will require adjustments in baking time.

9. Allow to cool before slicing or eating.

Reuben Sandwich

This sandwich is the king of the all-American delicatessen: home-baked rye bread (page 58) grilled in butter, dripping with rich cheese and Russian dressing, piled high with corned beef. It towers above the common sandwich. But Reuben's no snob, so lose the wine—cold beer is the perfect accompaniment.

Makes 1 sandwich

1 teaspoon butter, plus more if needed
2 slices rye or pumpernickel bread
2 teaspoons Russian dressing
1 ounce thinly sliced Emmenthaler or Swiss cheese
2 ounces thinly sliced corned beef
2 tablespoons well-drained sauerkraut

1. Butter 1 side of each slice of bread. Place 1 slice of bread, butter-side down, in a skillet. Spread 1 teaspoon of Russian dressing on the face-up side of the bread.

2. Cover with half the cheese, then the corned beef and sauerkraut. Finish with the other half of the cheese.

3. Spread the remaining Russian dressing on the dry side of the second slice of bread to complete the sandwich.

4. Place the skillet over medium-low heat and grill slowly for approximately 4 minutes per side, or until browned and crisp. Add additional butter to the pan if needed.

Caraway Swirl Rye

This bread has a pleasing appearance and taste that will really appeal to caraway lovers. An extra dose of caraway is swirled through the bread, producing a beautiful and flavorful crunch.

Makes 1 Caraway Swirl Rye

1 pound (grapefruit-size portion) Deli-Style Rye dough (page 58)
2 tablespoons caraway seeds, plus more for sprinkling on the top
Cornmeal for the pizza peel
Cornstarch wash (see page 51)

1. Dust the surface of the refrigerated dough with flour and cut off a 1-pound (grapefruit-size) piece. Dust the piece with more flour and quickly shape it into a ball by stretching the surface of the dough around to the bottom on all four sides, rotating the ball a quarter-turn as you go. Using your hands and a rolling pin, flatten the ball into a ½-inch-thick oval (avoid using extra flour here or it might remain as a dry deposit in the caraway swirl).

2. Sprinkle the dough with caraway seeds. The amount can vary with your taste; save some for the top crust. Then roll up the dough from the short end like a jelly roll, forming a cylindrical loaf. Pinch the ends closed.

3. Allow to rest for 1 hour and 20 minutes (or just 40 minutes if you're using fresh, unrefrigerated dough).

4. **Twenty minutes before baking time, preheat the oven to 450°F,** with a baking stone placed on the middle rack. Place an empty broiler tray on any other shelf that won't interfere with the rising bread.

5. Using a pastry brush, paint the top crust with cornstarch wash and

then sprinkle with the additional caraway seeds. Slash with deep parallel cuts across the loaf, using a serrated bread knife.

6. Slide the loaf directly onto the hot stone. Pour 1 cup of hot tap water into the broiler tray, and quickly close the oven door. Bake for 30 to 35 minutes, or until deeply browned and firm. Smaller or larger loaves will require adjustments in baking time.

7. Allow to cool before slicing or eating.

Onion Rye

The sweetness and aroma of sautéed onion go well with the flavor of rye. The onion needs to be sautéed until brown to bring out the caramelization that makes this bread so interesting. This recipe can be made using the standard Deli-Style Rye (page 58), with or without caraway seeds. Ordinary yellow or white onions work well and are readily available, but Vidalia or red varieties produce a milder onion flavor that some will prefer.

Makes 1 Onion Rye

Use any of these refrigerated pre-mixed doughs: Deli-Style Rye (page 58) or
   Pumpernickel (page 67)
1 pound (grapefruit-size portion) of any pre-mixed dough listed above
1 medium onion, halved and sliced thinly
Vegetable oil for sautéing the onions
Cornmeal for the pizza peel
Cornstarch wash (see sidebar, page 51)

1. Sauté the onions in the oil over medium heat for 10 minutes, or until brown.

2. Dust the surface of the refrigerated dough with flour and cut off a 1-pound (grapefruit-size) piece of dough. Dust the piece with more flour and quickly shape it into a ball by stretching the surface of the dough around to the bottom on all four sides, rotating the ball a quarter-turn as you go. Flatten the ball into a half-inch-thick oval either with your hands or a rolling pin (avoid using much extra flour here or it might remain as a dry deposit).

3. Spread the surface of the flattened loaf with a thin layer of the browned onion. Then roll up the dough from the short end like a jelly roll, forming a log.

4. Allow to rest and rise for 1 hour and 20 minutes (or just 40 minutes if you're using fresh, unrefrigerated dough).

5. **Twenty minutes before baking time, preheat the oven to 450°F,** with a baking stone placed on the middle rack. Place an empty broiler tray on any other shelf that won't interfere with the rising bread.

6. Using a pastry brush, paint the top crust with cornstarch wash. Slash with deep parallel cuts across the loaf, using a serrated bread knife.

7. Slide the loaf directly onto the hot stone. Pour 1 cup of hot tap water into the broiler tray, and quickly close the oven door. Bake for 30 to 35 minutes, until deeply browned and firm. Smaller or larger loaves will require adjustments in baking time.

8. Allow to cool before slicing or eating.

Limpa

Here's a five-minutes-a-day version of a traditional Scandinavian comfort food. Honey and orange zest blend with the more exotic flavors of anise and cardamom in this delicious Swedish bread.

Make two loaves; the first loaf will go quickly and you can use the second one in our bread pudding recipe, page 234.

Makes four 1-pound loaves. The recipe is easily doubled or halved.

3 cups lukewarm water
1½ tablespoons granulated yeast (1½ packets)
1½ tablespoons salt
½ cup honey
½ teaspoon ground anise seed
1 teaspoon ground cardamom
1½ teaspoons orange zest
1 cup rye flour
5½ cups unbleached all-purpose flour
Cornstarch wash (see sidebar, page 51)
Additionally, for each finished loaf you'll need ¼ teaspoon ground anise seed,
    ¼ teaspoon ground cardamom, plus 1½ teaspoons sugar mixed together
    for sprinkling on the top crust

1. **Mixing and storing the dough:** Mix the yeast, salt, honey, spices, and orange zest with the water in a 5-quart bowl, or a lidded (not airtight) food container.

2. Mix in the remaining dry ingredients without kneading, using a spoon, a 14-cup capacity food processor (with dough attachment), or a heavy-duty stand mixer (with dough hook). If you're not using a machine, you may need to use wet hands to incorporate the last bit of flour.

3. Cover (not airtight), and allow to rest at room temperature until dough rises and collapses (or flattens on top), approximately 2 hours.

4. The dough can be used immediately after the initial rise, though it is easier to handle when cold. Refrigerate in a lidded (not airtight) container and use over the next 7 days.

5. **On baking day**, dust the surface of the refrigerated dough with flour and cut off a 1-pound (grapefruit-size) piece. Dust the piece with more flour and quickly shape it into a ball by stretching the surface of the dough around to the bottom on all four sides, rotating the ball a quarter-turn as you go. Allow to rest and rise on a whole wheat–covered pizza peel for 40 minutes.

6. **Twenty minutes before baking time, preheat the oven to 375°F**, with a baking stone placed on the middle rack. Place an empty broiler tray on any other shelf that won't interfere with the rising bread.

7. Paint the surface with cornstarch wash and slash a cross, "scallop," or tic-tac-toe pattern into the top, using a serrated bread knife (see photo, page 29). Sprinkle with the additional anise, cardamom, and sugar mixture.

8. Slide the loaf directly onto the hot stone. Pour 1 cup of hot tap water into the broiler tray, and quickly close the oven door. Bake for about 40 minutes, or until golden brown and firm. Smaller or larger loaves will require adjustments in baking time. Due to the honey, the crust on this bread will not be hard and crackling.

9. Allow to cool before slicing or eating.

Pumpernickel Bread

Pumpernickel bread is really just a variety of rye bread. What darkens the loaf and accounts for its mildly bitter but appealing flavor is powdered caramel coloring, cocoa, molasses, and coffee, not the flour. The caramel color is actually a natural ingredient made by overheating sugar until it is completely caramelized (it's available from King Arthur Flour at www.kingarthurflour.com/shop/). Very traditional recipes use pumpernickel flour (a coarse rye with lots of rye bran), but this grain doesn't do well in our recipes because it absorbs water unpredictably. Since it's really the caramel, coffee, and chocolate that give pumpernickel its unique flavor and color, we successfully created a pumpernickel bread *without* true pumpernickel flour.

Altus: Many traditional pumpernickel recipes call for the addition of *"altus,"* which is stale rye or pumpernickel bread crumbs, soaked in water and blended into the dough. If you want to find a use for some stale rye or pumpernickel bread, you can experiment with this approach, which some say adds moisture and flavor to many traditional rye breads. Add up to a cup to the liquid ingredients before the flours. Adjust the flours to end up with dough of your usual consistency (you may need to adjust).

This bread is associated with Russia and caviar. If you're partial to caviar, here's your chance. Or just pile on the pastrami and corned beef!

Makes four 1-pound loaves. The recipe is easily doubled or halved.

3 cups lukewarm water
1½ tablespoons granulated yeast (1½ packets)
1½ tablespoons salt
2 tablespoons molasses
1½ tablespoons unsweetened cocoa powder
2 teaspoons instant espresso powder or instant coffee (or substitute brewed coffee for 2 cups of the water, keeping the total volume at 3 cups)

1½ tablespoons caramel color
1 cup rye flour
5½ cups unbleached all-purpose flour
Cornmeal for the pizza peel
Whole caraway seeds for sprinkling on the top, optional
Cornstarch wash (see sidebar, page 51)

1. **Mixing and storing the dough:** Mix the yeast, salt, molasses, cocoa, espresso powder, and caramel color with the water in the a 5-quart bowl, or a lidded (not airtight) food container.

2. Mix in the flours without kneading, using a spoon, a 14-cup capacity food processor (with dough attachment), or a heavy-duty stand mixer (with dough hook). If you're not using a machine, you may need to use wet hands to incorporate the last bit of flour.

3. Cover (not airtight), and allow to rest at room temperature until the dough rises and collapses (or flattens on top), approximately 2 hours.

4. The dough can be used immediately after the initial rise, though it is easier to handle when cold. Refrigerate in a lidded (not airtight) container and use over the next 8 days.

5. **On baking day,** cut off a 1-pound (grapefruit-size) piece of dough. Using wet hands (don't use flour), quickly shape the dough into a ball by stretching the surface of the dough around to the bottom on all four sides, rotating the ball a quarter-turn as you go. Then form an oval-shaped loaf. Allow to rest and rise on a cornmeal-covered pizza peel for 40 minutes.

6. **Twenty minutes before baking time, preheat the oven to 400°F,** with a baking stone placed on the middle rack. Place an empty broiler tray on any other shelf that won't interfere with the rising bread.

7. Using a pastry brush, paint the top crust with cornstarch wash and sprinkle with the caraway seeds, if using. Slash the loaf with deep parallel cuts, using a serrated bread knife (see photo, page 29).

8. Slide the loaf directly onto the hot stone. Pour 1 cup of hot tap water into the broiler tray, and quickly close the oven door. Bake for 35 to 40 minutes, until firm. Smaller or larger loaves will require adjustments in baking time.

9. Allow to cool before slicing or eating.

Pumpernickel Date and Walnut Bread

The sweetness of the dried fruit and the richness of the nuts are wonderful with the aromatic pumpernickel dough. We finish this loaf with nothing but the traditional cornstarch wash, letting the flavor of the fruit and nuts come through.

Makes 1 loaf

1 pound (grapefruit size portion) Pumpernickel Bread dough (page 67)
¼ cup chopped walnuts
¼ cup chopped dates or raisins
Cornmeal for the pizza peel
Cornstarch wash (see sidebar, page 51)

1. **On baking day,** using wet hands instead of flour, cut off a 1-pound (grapefruit-size) piece of dough. Continuing with wet hands, quickly shape the dough into a ball by stretching the surface of the dough around to the bottom on all four sides, rotating the ball a quarter-turn as you go.

2. Flatten the dough with your wet hands to a thickness of ½ inch and sprinkle with the walnuts and dates. Roll up the dough from the short end, like a jelly roll, to form a log. Using wet hands, crimp the ends shut and tuck them under to form an oval loaf.

3. Allow to rest and rise on a cornmeal-covered pizza peel for 1 hour and 40 minutes (or just 40 minutes if you're using fresh, unrefrigerated dough).

4. **Twenty minutes before baking time, preheat the oven to 400°F,** with a baking stone placed on the middle rack. Place an empty broiler tray on any other shelf that won't interfere with the rising bread.

5. Using a pastry brush, paint the top crust with cornstarch wash and then slash the loaf with deep parallel cuts, using a serrated bread knife (see photo, page 29).

6. Slide the loaf directly onto the hot stone. Pour 1 cup of hot tap water into the broiler tray, and quickly close the oven door. Bake for 35 to 40 minutes, until firm. Smaller or larger loaves will require adjustments in baking time.

7. Allow to cool before slicing or eating.

Bran-Enriched White Bread

There's no point in belaboring the value of bran in the diet. Cup for cup, wheat bran is much higher in fiber than whole wheat flour, yet it doesn't change the taste of bread as much as whole wheat flour. For those who don't care for the pleasantly bitter, nutty flavor of whole wheat, this loaf can serve as a mild-tasting, high-fiber substitute.

Makes four 1-pound loaves. The recipe is easily doubled or halved.

3 cups lukewarm water
1½ tablespoons granulated yeast (1½ packets)
1½ tablespoons salt
¾ cup wheat bran
5¾ cups unbleached all-purpose flour
Cornmeal for the pizza peel
Cornstarch wash (see sidebar, page 51)

1. **Mixing and storing the dough:** Mix the yeast and salt with the water in a 5-quart bowl, or a lidded (not airtight) food container.

2. Mix in the remaining dry ingredients without kneading, using a spoon, a 14-cup capacity food processor (with dough attachment), or a heavy-duty stand mixer (with dough hook). If you're not using a machine, you may need to use wet hands to incorporate the last bit of flour.

3. Allow to rest at room temperature until the dough rises and collapses (or flattens on top), approximately 2 hours.

4. The dough can be used immediately after the initial rise, though it is easier to handle when cold. Refrigerate in a lidded (not airtight) container and use over the next 14 days.

5. **On baking day**, dust the surface of the refrigerated dough with flour

and cut off a 1-pound (grapefruit-size) piece. Dust the piece with more flour and quickly shape it into a ball by stretching the surface of the dough around to the bottom on all four sides, rotating the ball a quarter-turn as you go. Then form an oval-shaped loaf. Allow to rest and rise on a cornmeal-covered pizza peel for 40 minutes.

6. **Twenty minutes before baking time, preheat the oven to 450°F,** with a baking stone placed on the middle rack. Place an empty broiler tray on any other shelf that won't interfere with the rising bread.

7. Sprinkle the loaf liberally with flour and slash parallel cuts across the loaf, using a serrated bread knife (see photo, page 29). Leave the flour in place for baking; tap some of it off before eating.

8. Slide the loaf directly onto the hot stone. Pour 1 cup of hot tap water into the broiler tray, and quickly close the oven door. Bake for about 30 minutes, until deeply browned and firm. Smaller or larger loaves will require adjustments in baking time.

9. Allow to cool before slicing or eating.

Light Whole Wheat Bread

You'll find this recipe a basic workhorse when you want a versatile and healthy light wheat bread for sandwiches, appetizers, and snacks. The blend of all-purpose flour and whole wheat creates a bread lighter in texture, taste, and appearance than our 100% Whole Wheat (page 76). Try them both and find your favorite.

Makes four 1-pound loaves. The recipe is easily doubled or halved.

3 cups lukewarm water
1½ tablespoons granulated yeast (1½ packets)
1½ tablespoons salt
1 cup whole wheat flour
5½ cups unbleached all-purpose flour
Whole wheat flour for the pizza peel

1. **Mixing and storing the dough:** Mix the yeast and salt with the water in a 5-quart bowl, or a lidded (not airtight) food container.

2. Mix in the remaining dry ingredients without kneading, using a spoon, a 14-cup capacity food processor (with dough attachment), or a heavy-duty stand mixer (with dough hook). If you're not using a machine, you may need to use wet hands to incorporate the last bit of flour.

3. Cover (not airtight), and allow to rest at room temperature until the dough rises and collapses (or flattens on top), approximately 2 hours.

4. The dough can be used immediately after the initial rise, though it is easier to handle when cold. Refrigerate in a lidded (not airtight) container and use over the next 14 days.

5. **On baking day,** dust the surface of the refrigerated dough with flour and cut off a 1-pound (grapefruit-size) piece. Dust the piece with

more flour and quickly shape it into a ball by stretching the surface of the dough around to the bottom on all four sides, rotating the ball a quarter-turn as you go. Allow to rest and rise on a cornmeal-covered pizza peel for 40 minutes.

6. **Twenty minutes before baking time, preheat the oven to 450°F,** with a baking stone placed on the middle rack. Place an empty broiler tray on any other shelf that won't interfere with the rising bread.

7. Sprinkle the loaf liberally with flour and slash a cross, "scallop," or tic-tac-toe pattern into the top, using a serrated bread knife (see photo, page 29). Leave the flour in place for baking; tap some of it off before eating.

8. Slide the loaf directly onto the hot stone. Pour 1 cup of hot tap water into the broiler tray, and quickly close the oven door. Bake for about 35 minutes, or until deeply browned and firm. Smaller or larger loaves will require adjustments in baking time.

9. Allow to cool before slicing or eating.

100% Whole Wheat Sandwich Bread

Whole wheat flour has a nutty, slightly bitter flavor, and it caramelizes very easily, yielding a rich, brown, and flavorful loaf. We've used milk and honey as tenderizers, but the honey's sweetness also makes a nice counterpoint to the whole wheat's bitter notes. Although we've showcased a loaf-pan method here, this dough also makes lovely free-form loaves using the baking stone.

Makes three 1½-pound loaves. The recipe is easily doubled or halved.

1½ cups lukewarm water
1½ cups lukewarm milk
1½ tablespoons granulated yeast (1½ packets)
1 tablespoon plus 1 teaspoon salt
½ cup honey
5 tablespoons neutral-flavored oil, plus more for greasing the pan
6⅔ cups whole wheat flour (avoid whole wheat pastry flour or "graham" flour)

1. **Mixing and storing the dough:** Mix the yeast, salt, honey, and oil with the milk and water in a 5-quart bowl, or a lidded (not airtight) food container.

2. Mix in the remaining dry ingredients without kneading, using a spoon, a 14-cup capacity food processor (with dough attachment), or a heavy-duty stand mixer (with dough hook).

3. Cover (not airtight), and allow to rest at room temperature until the dough rises and collapses (or flattens on top); approximately 2 to 3 hours.

4. The dough can be used immediately after the initial rise, though it is easier to handle when cold. Refrigerate in a lidded (not airtight) container and use over the next 5 days.

5. **On baking day,** lightly grease a 9×4×3-inch nonstick loaf pan. Using wet hands, scoop out a 1½-pound (cantaloupe-size) handful of dough. This dough is pretty sticky and often it's easiest to handle it with wet hands. Keeping your hands wet, quickly shape it into a ball by stretching the surface of the dough around to the bottom on all four sides, rotating the ball a quarter-turn as you go.

6. Drop the loaf into the prepared pan. You want to fill the pan slightly more than half-full.

7. Allow the dough to rest for 1 hour and 40 minutes. Flour the top of the loaf and slash, using the tip of a serrated bread knife.

8. **Twenty minutes before baking time, preheat the oven to 350°F,** with an empty broiler tray on any other shelf that won't interfere with the rising bread. If you're not using a stone, the preheat can be as short as 5 minutes.

9. Place the loaf on a rack near the center of the oven. Pour 1 cup of hot tap water into the broiler tray and quickly close the oven door. Bake for 50 to 60 minutes, or until deeply browned and firm.

10. Allow to cool completely before slicing in order to cut reasonable sandwich slices.

Whole Wheat Sandwich Bread Inspired by Chris Kimball

Chris Kimball publishes *Cook's Magazine*, and has written a number of wonderful common-sense cookbooks celebrating American regional home-cooking. As Chris has written, home chefs can produce honest and authentic but simple versions of what the best artisan chefs spend a lifetime perfecting. We agree, and that's part of the idea behind this book: authentic but simple.

In 1997, Chris developed a whole wheat bread recipe in the soft-crusted American style, and ran it in *Cook's Magazine*. We've adapted it here for stored high-moisture dough and we think you'll enjoy the delicious effect created by the wheat germ, rye, and honey. Even though this bread is soft-crusted, we bake it with steam because it improves the color and appearance.

Makes three 1½-pound loaves. The recipe is easily doubled or halved.

3 cups lukewarm water
1½ tablespoons granulated yeast (1½ packets)
1 tablespoon plus 1 teaspoon salt
¼ cup honey
¼ cup unsalted butter, melted
¼ cup rye flour
½ cup wheat germ
2¾ cups whole wheat flour
2¾ cups unbleached all-purpose flour
Neutral-tasting oil for greasing the pan

1. **Mixing and storing the dough:** Mix the yeast, salt, honey, and butter with the lukewarm water in a 5-quart bowl, or a lidded (not airtight) food container.

2. Mix in the remaining dry ingredients without kneading, using a spoon, a 14-cup capacity food processor (with dough attachment), or a heavy-duty stand mixer (with dough hook). If you're not using a machine, you may need to use wet hands to incorporate the last bit of flour.

3. Cover (not airtight), and allow to rest at room temperature until the dough rises and collapses (or flattens on top); approximately 2 hours.

4. The dough can be used immediately after the initial rise, though it is easier to handle when cold. Refrigerate in a lidded (not airtight) container and use over the next 5 days.

5. **On baking day,** lightly grease a 9×4×3-inch nonstick loaf pan. Dust the surface of the refrigerated dough with flour and cut off a 1½-pound (cantaloupe-size) piece. Dust the piece with more flour and quickly shape it into a ball by stretching the surface of the dough around to the bottom on all four sides, rotating the ball a quarter-turn as you go. Form an elongated oval and place it into the prepared pan. Allow to rest for 1 hour and 40 minutes (or just 40 minutes if you're using fresh, unrefrigerated dough).

6. **Twenty minutes before baking time, preheat the oven to 400°F,** with an empty broiler tray on any other shelf that won't interfere with the rising bread.

7. Place the loaf on a rack near the center of the oven. Pour 1 cup of hot tap water into the broiler tray and quickly close the oven door. Bake for about 50 minutes, or until deeply browned and firm.

8. Allow to cool before slicing or eating.

Italian Semolina Bread

White, free-form loaves flavored with semolina and sesame seeds are the fragrant products of southern Italy. Semolina is a high-protein wheat flour that gives loaves a sweetness, and an almost winey aroma. In our minds, the flavor of the sesame seeds is inextricably linked to the semolina flavor (like caraway and rye). Be sure to use semolina flour that's labeled "durum," other semolina flours won't do as well in our method.

Makes four 1-pound loaves. The recipe is easily doubled or halved.

3 cups lukewarm water
1½ tablespoons granulated yeast (1½ packets)
1½ tablespoons salt
3 cups durum flour
3¼ cups unbleached all-purpose flour
Sesame seeds for top crust, approximately 1 to 2 teaspoons
Cornmeal for the pizza peel
Cornstarch wash (see sidebar, page 51)

1. **Mixing and storing the dough:** Mix the yeast and salt with the lukewarm water in a 5-quart bowl, or a lidded (not airtight) food container.

2. Mix in the flours without kneading, using a spoon, a 14-cup capacity food processor (with dough attachment), or a heavy-duty stand mixer (with dough hook). If you're not using a machine, you may need to use wet hands to incorporate the last bit of flour.

3. Cover (not airtight), and allow to rest at room temperature until the dough rises and collapses (or flattens on top), approximately 2 hours.

4. The dough can be used immediately after the initial rise, though it is easier to handle when cold. Refrigerate in a lidded (not airtight) container and use over the next 14 days.

5. **On baking day**, dust the surface of the refrigerated dough with flour and cut off a 1-pound (grapefruit-size) piece. Dust the piece with more flour and quickly shape it into a ball by stretching the surface of the dough around to the bottom on all four sides, rotating the ball a quarter-turn as you go. Elongate the ball to form an oval-shaped free-form loaf. Allow to rest and rise on a cornmeal-covered pizza peel for 40 minutes.

6. **Twenty minutes before baking time, preheat the oven to 450°F,** with a baking stone placed on the middle rack. Place an empty broiler tray on any other shelf that won't interfere with the rising bread.

7. Just before baking, paint the surface with cornstarch wash, sprinkle with sesame seeds, and slash the surface diagonally, using a serrated bread knife.

8. Slide the loaf directly onto the hot stone. Pour 1 cup of hot tap water into the broiler tray, and quickly close the oven door. Bake for 30 to 35 minutes, until deeply browned and firm. Smaller or larger loaves will require adjustments in baking time.

9. Allow to cool before slicing or eating.

Broa (Portuguese Corn Bread)

Broa is a very rustic recipe from the Portuguese countryside. *Broa* just means bread in Portuguese, but it's often used to refer specifically to this dense part-corn loaf that's perfect for sopping up hearty soups like our Portuguese Fish Stew (page 84). It bears little resemblance to American Southern corn-bread, which is quite sweet, and leavened with baking soda and powder.

Form this loaf as a relatively flattened ball (so that you'll get lots of crust). The flattened loaf is truer to the original and helps to prevent dense-ness from the corn.

Makes four 1-pound loaves. The recipe is easily doubled or halved.

3 cups lukewarm water
1½ tablespoons granulated yeast (1½ packets)
1½ tablespoons salt
1½ cups stone-ground or standard cornmeal
5 cups unbleached all-purpose flour
Cornmeal for pizza peel and dusting the top

1. **Mixing and storing the dough:** Mix the yeast and salt with the water in a 5-quart bowl, or a lidded (not airtight) food container.

2. Mix in the remaining dry ingredients without kneading, using a spoon, a 14-cup capacity food processor (with dough attachment), or a heavy-duty stand mixer (with dough hook). If you're not using a machine, you may need to use wet hands to incorporate the last bit of flour.

3. Cover (not airtight), and allow to rest at room temperature until the dough rises and collapses (or flattens on top), approximately 2 hours.

4. The dough can be used immediately after the initial rise, though it is easier to handle when cold. Refrigerate in a lidded (not airtight) container and use over the next 10 days.

5. **On baking day,** dust the surface of the refrigerated dough with flour and cut off a 1-pound (grapefruit-size) piece. Dust the piece with more flour and quickly shape it into a ball by stretching the surface of the dough around to the bottom on all four sides, rotating the ball a quarter-turn as you go. Flatten slightly and allow to rest and rise on a cornmeal-covered pizza peel for 40 minutes.

6. **Twenty minutes before baking time, preheat a baking stone to 450°F,** with a baking stone placed on the middle rack. Place an empty broiler tray on any other shelf that won't interfere with the rising bread.

7. Just before baking, sprinkle the loaf liberally with cornmeal and slash a cross, "scallop," or tic-tac-toe pattern into the top, using a serrated bread knife (see photo, page 29). Leave the cornmeal in place for baking; tap some of it off before eating.

8. Slide the loaf directly onto the hot stone. Pour 1 cup of hot tap water into the broiler tray, and quickly close the oven door. Bake for about 30 minutes, until deeply browned and firm. Smaller or larger loaves will require adjustments in baking time.

9. Allow to cool before slicing or eating.

Portuguese Fish Stew (Caldeirada de Peixe)

We include this simple and delicious recipe that was born to have *Broa* (page 82) dipped into it. The distinguishing character of this soup comes from the orange zest and hot pepper, which makes it quite different from French or Italian versions. Cod is a typical Portuguese choice to include, but the dish works well with any combination of boneless white-fleshed, non-oily fish, and/or shellfish.

Makes 6 to 8 servings

¼ cup olive oil
1 large onion, chopped
2 leeks, washed to remove interior soil and coarsely chopped
1 bulb fennel, white parts only, coarsely chopped
5 finely chopped garlic cloves
1 cup diced tomatoes, canned or fresh
1 red bell pepper, cored, seeded, and diced
1 bay leaf
Zest of 1 orange
1 quart fish stock or water, or an 8-ounce bottle of clam juice plus 3 cups
    water
2 cups dry white wine
Scant ¼ teaspoon hot red pepper flakes
1 tablespoon salt
Freshly ground pepper to taste
3 pounds mixed white, non-oily boneless fish and shellfish, or just fish

1. Heat the oil in a large stockpot, add the onions and leeks, and sauté in olive oil until softened. Add the fennel and garlic and sauté until aromatic.

2. Add all the remaining ingredients except the fish and shellfish and bring to a boil. Cover, lower heat, and simmer for 20 minutes.

3. While the stock is simmering, cut the fish into bite-size portions. Bring the stock back to a rapid boil, add the fish, and cook for 1 minute.

4. Add the shellfish (if using) and continue to boil until shells open, approximately 1 minute. Shake the pan occasionally to encourage clam and mussel shells to open. If using shrimp, turn off the heat as soon as all the shrimp lose their gray translucency; any longer and they quickly become tough and overcooked. Depending on your pot and burner, this will probably be about 2 to 3 minutes.

5. Serve hot with wedges of *Broa* (page 82).

Yeasted Thanksgiving Corn Bread with Cranberries

Traditional American corn bread is a butter or lard-enriched quick bread, risen with baking powder and baking soda. We make ours with yeasted *Broa* dough (page 82). For a Thanksgiving feel, we studded the dough with sweetened cranberries. Playing on the American corn bread theme, we baked the loaf in a heated cast-iron pan, liberally greased with butter, lard, bacon grease, or oil, creating a rich and flavorful crust.

Like a baking stone, cast iron absorbs a lot of energy when its temperature rises in an oven, retains heat well, and radiates it very evenly to the dough, promoting a nice brown crust. Though cast iron can't absorb moisture, it makes the baking stone optional here.

Makes 1 corn bread

1½ pounds *Broa* dough (page 82) approximately 1 cantaloupe-size handful,
   or enough to fill a 12-inch cast-iron pan to a depth of about 1½ inches
½ cup fresh cranberries or ⅓ cup dried
4 tablespoons sugar
Zest of half an orange
3 tablespoons softened butter, lard, bacon grease, or neutral-tasting oil for
   greasing the pan

1. Dust the surface of the refrigerated dough with flour and cut off a
   1½-pound (cantaloupe-size) piece. Dust the piece with more flour
   and quickly shape it into a ball by stretching the surface of the dough
   around to the bottom on all four sides, rotating the ball a quarter-turn
   as you go.

2. Flatten the ball with your hands to a thickness of ½ inch. Sprinkle the
   dough with the cranberries, sugar, and orange zest. Roll up the dough
   from the short end, jelly-roll style, to incorporate the cranberries.
   Shape into a ball again, then flatten until it is about the size of your
   pan.

3. Grease a cast-iron pan with all of the butter, lard, bacon grease, or oil, being sure to coat the sides of the pan as well. Place the dough into the pan. Allow the dough to rest for 1 hour and 20 minutes (or just 40 minutes if you're using fresh, unrefrigerated dough).

4. **Twenty minutes before baking time, preheat the oven to 425°F,** and place a broiler tray for water on any other shelf that won't interfere with the rising bread. A baking stone is optional here given the use of a cast-iron pan. If you omit the stone, the preheat can be as short as 5 minutes.

5. Just before baking, heat the cast-iron pan over medium heat for 1 or 2 minutes to jump-start the baking process and promote caramelization of the bottom crust (don't overdo it—no more than 2 minutes).

6. Place the pan on a rack near the center of the oven. Pour 1 cup of hot tap water into the broiler tray and quickly close the oven door. Check for browning in about 20 minutes. The time required will depend on the size and weight of pan but will probably be about 30 minutes. The loaf should be a rich yellow-brown when done.

7. Carefully turn the hot loaf out of the pan onto a serving plate, or just cut wedges directly out of the pan.

Spicy Pork Buns

We'd been searching for a simple way to re-create and reconstruct some of the flavor combinations in great tamales. Here's a simple recipe combining the sweet flavor of corn from the *Broa* dough, meat, and two kinds of chili peppers. It's a bit more time-consuming than our other recipes, but worth it.

Children devour these, but if your kids won't eat spicy food, you may want to tone down the *chipotles en adobo*, or leave them out altogether. We serve this dish as a main course, with added sauce on the side. You can put more sauce inside the buns, but don't overdo it or the result may be soggy.

Makes 4 large buns

The Meat Filling

1 to 1½ cups of cooked meat from a pork roast (shoulder or butt) or beef brisket

One 28-ounce can crushed tomatoes

2 chipotle peppers from a can of *chipotles en adobo*, finely chopped

2 dried chili peppers (New Mexico red, *guajillo*, or *ancho* variety), or substitute 1 tablespoon of your favorite chili powder

1 medium onion

1½ teaspoons cumin seeds

2 teaspoons salt

1 teaspoon cornstarch

2 tablespoons chopped fresh cilantro

The Wrappers

1 pound (grapefruit-size portion) *Broa* dough (page 82)

1. **Make the meat filling:** *If you're grinding your own chili pepper:* Briefly toast the dried peppers in a 400°F oven until fragrant but not burned, 1 to 2 minutes (they'll remain flexible). Break up the toasted peppers and discard the stems and seeds. Grind with the cumin seeds in a spice grinder (or coffee grinder used just for spices).

2. Trim the meat of hardened fat; shred with knife, fork, and your fingers, pulling strips off the roast or brisket along the direction of the grain.

3. Place all ingredients for the meat filling except the cornstarch and cilantro in a roomy pot on the stove top. The pot should be large enough to hold the meat and still allow the cover to seal. The liquid should not come higher than about one-third of the way up the meat. Bring to a simmer and cook, covered, until very soft, approximately 3 hours, turning occasionally. Separate the meat and sauce and chill in the refrigerator.

4. When chilled, skim the fat from the surface of the sauce. Anytime before assembling the buns, reheat the meat mixture. Mix the cornstarch with a small amount of sauce in a little cup to make a paste; then add to the pot. Simmer for 2 minutes, or until thickened.

5. **Preheat the oven to 450°F**, with a baking stone set in the middle of the oven. Place a broiler tray for holding water on any other shelf that won't interfere with the rising bread.

6. Dust the surface of the refrigerated dough with flour and cut off a 1-pound (grapefruit-size) piece. Divide the dough into four equal balls. Briefly shape, flattening out each ball with your fingers. Using a rolling pin, roll out 8- to 10-inch rounds about ⅛ inch thick or less. Use minimal white flour on your work surface as you roll so that the dough sticks to it a bit.

7. **Assemble the buns:** Place approximately 4 tablespoons of shredded meat in the center of each round of dough. Add about a tablespoon of sauce and ½ tablespoon of chopped cilantro. Wet the edges of the dough round with water. Gather the edges of the dough around the meat, pinching at the center to form a seal; you may need to use a dough scraper to pull up sections of the wrapper.

8. Using a dough scraper, if necessary, remove the finished buns from the work surface and place on a cornmeal-covered pizza peel. No resting time is needed.

9. Slide the buns directly onto the hot stone. Pour 1 cup of hot tap water into the broiler tray, and quickly close the oven door. Check for browning in 15 minutes and continue baking until the buns are medium brown.

10. Serve immediately, with additional sauce, and Mexican hot pepper sauce.

English Granary-Style Bread

The English have created a great new cuisine based on superfresh local ingredients, and Jamie Oliver's books have led the way. We've adapted a simple green salad of his based on watercress (page 93), the quintessential British green; Jamie's salad adds a twist on the traditional English watercress salad.

But when it comes to English bread, we're traditionalists. To accompany those new dishes, here is a staple of the *old* village bakery: a multigrain loaf that includes malted wheat and barley. The combination of grains create a slightly sweet and comforting flavor. Malted wheat flakes and malt powder can be ordered from King Arthur Flour (www.kingarthurflour.com/shop/).

Makes four 1-pound loaves. The recipe is easily doubled or halved.

3¼ cups lukewarm water
1½ tablespoons granulated yeast (1½ packets)
1½ tablespoons salt
¼ cup malt powder
1 cup malted wheat flakes
1 cup whole wheat flour
5 cups unbleached all-purpose flour
Cornmeal for the pizza peel
Cornstarch wash (see sidebar, page 51)
1 tablespoon cracked wheat, for sprinkling on top crust

1. **Mixing and storing the dough:** Mix the yeast, salt, and malt powder with the lukewarm water in a 5-quart bowl, or a lidded (not airtight) food container.

2. Mix in the wheat flakes and the flours without kneading, using a spoon, a 14-cup capacity food processor (with dough attachment), or a heavy-duty stand mixer (with dough hook). If you're not using a machine, you may need to use wet hands to incorporate the last bit of flour.

3. Cover (not airtight), and allow to rest at room temperature until the dough rises and collapses (or flattens on top), approximately 2 hours.

4. The dough can be used immediately after the initial rise, though it is easier to handle when cold. Refrigerate in a lidded (not airtight) container and use over the next 10 days.

5. **On baking day,** dust the surface of the refrigerated dough with flour and cut off a 1-pound (grapefruit-size) piece. Dust the piece with more flour and quickly shape it into a ball by stretching the surface of the dough around to the bottom on all four sides, rotating the ball a quarter-turn as you go. Allow to rest and rise on a cornmeal-covered pizza peel for 40 minutes.

6. **Twenty minutes before baking time, preheat the oven to 400°F,** with a baking stone placed on the middle rack. Place an empty broiler tray on any other shelf that won't interfere with the rising bread.

7. Brush the loaf with cornstarch wash and sprinkle with cracked wheat. Slash a cross or a tic-tac-toe pattern into the top, using a serrated bread knife (see photo, page 29).

8. Slide the loaf directly onto the hot stone. Pour 1 cup of hot tap water into the broiler tray, and quickly close the oven door. Bake for about 35 minutes. Smaller or larger loaves will require adjustments in baking time.

9. Allow to cool before slicing.

Jamie Oliver's Watercress, Rocket, Sweet Pear, Walnut, and Parmesan Salad

Here's a fantastic salad from Jamie Oliver's marvelous cookbook *The Return of the Naked Chef*. The recipe matches our quick and fresh approach to eating. Jamie loves to measure with "handfuls," "squeezes," and "drizzles," so we did, too.

Serves 4

2 pears, cored, halved, and sliced
4 handfuls watercress
4 handfuls rocket (arugula)
Extra virgin olive oil
Fresh lemon juice
Coarse salt to taste
Freshly ground black pepper to taste
Parmigiano-Reggiano or pecorino cheese for grating over salad
Handful of walnuts

1. Put pears and greens into a salad bowl.

2. Drizzle with good extra virgin olive oil just to coat, add a small squeeze of lemon juice, and season well with salt and freshly ground black pepper.

3. Toss well and place on 4 plates. Shave some Parmesan or pecorino cheese over the salad, and sprinkle with some walnuts.

Oatmeal Bread

This lightly sweetened and hearty bread tastes great straight from the oven with butter and cinnamon-sugar. It also makes a great sandwich with smoked turkey and cheese. Or serve it with Laura's Three-Citrus Marmalade (page 96).

Makes three 1½-pound loaves. The recipe is easily doubled or halved.

1¾ cups lukewarm water
1 cup whole milk
½ cup pure maple syrup
1½ tablespoons granulated yeast (1½ packets)
1 tablespoon salt
¼ cup neutral-tasting oil, plus more for greasing the pan
½ cup oat bran
⅓ cup wheat bran
1½ cups old-fashioned rolled oats
½ cup whole wheat flour
4¼ cups unbleached all-purpose flour

1. **Mixing and storing the dough:** Mix the yeast and salt with the water, milk, maple syrup, and oil in a 5-quart bowl, or a lidded (not airtight) food container.

2. Mix in the remaining dry ingredients without kneading, using a spoon, a 14-cup capacity food processor (with dough attachment), or a heavy-duty stand mixer (with dough hook). If you're not using a machine, you may need to use wet hands to incorporate the last bit of flour.

3. Cover (not airtight), and allow to rest at room temperature until the dough rises and collapses (or flattens on top), approximately 2 hours.

4. The dough can be used immediately after the initial rise, though it is easier to handle when cold. Refrigerate in a lidded (not airtight) container and use over the next 8 days.

5. **On baking day,** lightly grease a 9×4×3-inch nonstick loaf pan. Dust the surface of the refrigerated dough with flour and cut off a 1½-pound (cantaloupe-size) piece. Dust the piece with more flour and quickly shape it into a ball by stretching the surface of the dough around to the bottom on all four sides, rotating the ball a quarter-turn as you go.

6. Elongate the ball into an oval and place it into the prepared pan. Allow to rest and rise for 1 hour and 20 minutes (or just 40 minutes if you're using fresh, unrefrigerated dough).

7. **Twenty minutes before baking time, preheat the oven to 350°F,** with an empty broiler tray on any other shelf that won't interfere with the rising bread.

8. Place the loaf on a rack near the center of the oven. Pour 1 cup of hot tap water into the broiler tray and quickly close the oven door. Bake for 45 to 50 minutes, or until deeply browned and firm.

9. Allow to cool before slicing or eating.

Laura's Three-Citrus Marmalade

Here's something sweet yet startlingly tart to put on your Oatmeal Bread (page 94), or just about anything else. Citrus can be had all year but, if you wait until the height of the season, the selection increases. Try substituting blood oranges or tangerines for the navel oranges when in season.

"My wife, Laura, does the canning at our house, and she makes a marmalade that everyone loves. I wish I could say that the recipe was whispered to her in an Italian citrus grove, but Laura enjoys telling foodies that it comes from the instruction sheet inside the Sure-Jell box. But she is too modest. Laura adapted Sure-Jell's orange marmalade by adding pink grapefruit, which brings a touch of extra tartness that makes the marmalade unique."—Jeff

If you're intimidated by canning, simply skip the sterilization procedure in the final step and refrigerate the marmalade for up to 2 months or freeze it for up to 1 year.

Makes 7 cups

4 navel oranges
1 lemon
½ pink grapefruit
2½ cups water
⅛ teaspoon baking soda
5½ cups sugar
1 box (1.75 ounces) Sure-Jell fruit pectin

1. Using a vegetable peeler, remove the colored zest from the fruit and discard the white pith. Chop the zest coarsely.

2. Chop the fruit, discarding any seeds and reserving the juice.

3. Place the zests, water, and baking soda into a saucepan and bring to a boil. Reduce heat; cover and simmer 20 minutes, stirring occasionally. Add fruit and juice; simmer another 10 minutes.

4. Measure the sugar and set aside. Do not reduce the sugar, or marmalade may not set properly.

5. Stir the box of fruit pectin into the fruit mixture. Bring to a full, rolling boil.

6. Stir in the sugar quickly, return to a full rolling boil, and cook for 1 minute. Remove from the heat and skim off any foam.

7. Pour the hot marmalade into clean canning jars. Process according to the canner and U.S. Department of Agriculture instructions, or refrigerate and use within 2 months. The marmalade also can be frozen, without canning, for up to 1 year.

Raisin-Walnut Oatmeal Bread

Full of the flavors we associate with oatmeal—raisins, walnuts, and a touch of maple syrup, this will remind you of the breakfast your mother made you when you were a kid. If not, it will be the breakfast your kids beg you to make.

Makes 1 loaf

Neutral-tasting oil for greasing the pan
1½ pounds (cantaloupe-size portion) Oatmeal Bread dough (page 94)
1 cup raisins
¾ cup walnuts
Egg wash (1 egg beaten with 1 tablespoon of water)

1. **On baking day,** lightly grease a 9×4×3-inch nonstick loaf pan. Dust the surface of the refrigerated dough with flour and cut off a 1½-pound (cantaloupe-size) piece. Dust the piece with more flour and quickly shape it into a ball by stretching the surface of the dough around to the bottom on all four sides, rotating the ball a quarter-turn as you go.

2. Flatten the dough with your hands and roll out into a ½-inch-thick rectangle. As you roll out the dough, use enough flour to prevent it from sticking to the work surface but not so much as to make the dough dry.

3. Sprinkle the raisins and walnuts over the dough and roll the dough up to encase them. Fold the dough over again and then shape to approximate a loaf shape, using a small amount of flour if necessary.

4. Place the loaf in the prepared pan, and allow to rest for approximately 1 hour and 40 minutes (or just 40 minutes if you're using fresh, unrefrigerated dough).

5. **Twenty minutes before baking time, preheat the oven to 350°F.** Brush the loaf with the egg wash. Bake for approximately 45 minutes or until golden brown.

6. Allow to cool before slicing or eating.

VARIATION:
Substitute 1 cup of chopped dried apricots for the raisins.

Oatmeal Pumpkin Bread

Here's a great use for leftover pumpkin puree, something that virtually never gets used up. Roasting the pumpkin caramelizes the sugars and intensifies the flavors, so it's worth the effort to do your own rather than substituting with canned pumpkin puree. If you do roast your own, be sure to use the smaller "pie" pumpkin and not the watery and flavorless decorative pumpkin.

"In the fall at my house, there is almost always a pumpkin roasting for pie and a batch of oatmeal cooking for breakfast. This is Minnesota and these are the things that keep us warm and happy. One day I had both going, and decided to try combining them into a bread. Well, it worked beautifully and is now one of my family's favorites. For obvious reasons I tend to make a lot of it right around Thanksgiving. It's perfect with leftover turkey."—Zoë

Makes three 1½-pound loaves. The recipe is easily doubled or halved.

1 pie pumpkin
2 cups lukewarm water
1½ tablespoons granulated yeast (1½ packets)
1 tablespoon salt
5 tablespoons unsalted butter, melted
⅓ cup honey
½ cup old-fashioned oats
¾ cup whole wheat flour
¾ cup rye flour
4 cups unbleached all-purpose flour
Neutral-tasting oil for greasing the pan

1. **Preheat the oven to 350°F.** Split the pumpkin in half starting at the stem and place cut side down on a silicone mat or a lightly greased cookie sheet. Bake for 45 minutes. The pumpkin should be very soft all the way through when poked with a knife. Cool slightly before scooping out the seeds.

2. Scoop out the roasted flesh of the pumpkin and mash it with a fork or

puree it in the food processor. Set aside 1 cup for the dough and use the rest in your favorite pie recipe.

3. **Mixing and storing the dough:** Mix the yeast and salt with the water, melted butter, and honey in a 5-quart bowl, or a lidded (not airtight) food container.

4. Mix in the oatmeal, pumpkin, and flours without kneading, using a spoon, a 14-cup capacity food processor (with dough attachment), or a heavy-duty stand mixer (with dough hook). If you're not using a machine, you may need to use wet hands to incorporate the last bit of flour.

5. Cover (not airtight), and allow to rest at room temperature until the dough rises and collapses (or flattens on top), approximately 2 hours.

6. The dough can be used immediately after the initial rise, though it is easier to handle when cold. Refrigerate in a lidded (not airtight) container and use over the next 9 days.

7. **On baking day,** lightly grease a 9×5×3-inch nonstick loaf pan. Dust the surface of the refrigerated dough with flour and cut off a 1½-pound (cantaloupe-size) piece. Dust the piece with more flour and quickly shape it into a ball by stretching the surface of the dough around to the bottom on all four sides, rotating the ball a quarter-turn as you go.

8. Place the dough in the prepared pan, and allow to rest and rise for 2 hours (or just 40 minutes if you're using fresh, unrefrigerated dough).

9. **Twenty minutes before baking time, preheat the oven to 350°F,** with an empty broiler tray for water on any other shelf that won't interfere with the rising bread.

10. Place the loaf on a rack near the center of the oven. Pour 1 cup of hot tap water into the broiler tray and quickly close the oven door. Bake for 45 to 50 minutes, or until deeply browned and firm.

11. Allow to cool before slicing or eating.

Oatmeal Pumpkin Seed Bread

To jazz up the Oatmeal Pumpkin Bread (page 100), roll in pumpkin seeds and dried cranberries. It adds both a sweet element and a tartness that is wonderful with the other flavors, and nothing could be more appropriate at Thanksgiving. You can buy pre-shelled toasted pumpkin seeds in most groceries, usually in the Mexican food aisle, where they might be labeled *pepitas*.

Makes 1 loaf

Neutral-tasting oil for greasing the pan
1½ pounds (cantaloupe-size portion) Oatmeal Pumpkin dough (page 100)
¼ cup hulled, toasted pumpkin seeds
¼ cup dried cranberries
Egg wash (one egg beaten with 1 tablespoon of water)

1. **On baking day,** lightly grease a 9×4×3-inch nonstick loaf pan. Dust the surface of the refrigerated dough with flour and cut off a 1½-pound (grapefruit-size) piece. Dust the piece with more flour and quickly shape it into a ball by stretching the surface of the dough around to the bottom on all four sides, rotating the ball a quarter-turn as you go.

2. Flatten the dough with your hands and roll out into a ½-inch-thick rectangle. As you roll out the dough, use enough flour to prevent it from sticking to the work surface but not so much as to make the dough dry.

3. Sprinkle the seeds and cranberries over the dough and roll the dough up to encase them. Fold the dough over again to work the seeds into the dough.

4. Using a small amount of flour, form the dough into a loaf shape. Place the loaf in the prepared pan and allow to rest and rise 2 hours (or just 40 minutes if you're using fresh, unrefrigerated dough).

5. **Twenty minutes before baking time, preheat the oven to 350°F,** and place an empty broiler tray on any other shelf that won't interfere with the rising bread. The baking stone is not essential for loaf pan breads; if you omit it the preheat may be as short as 5 minutes.

6. Just before putting the bread in the oven, brush the loaf with egg wash and place it on a rack near the center of the oven. Pour 1 cup of hot tap water into the broiler tray and quickly close the oven door. Bake the loaf for 45 to 50 minutes, until deeply browned and firm.

7. Allow to cool before slicing or eating.

Oat Flour Bread

If you're looking for a delicious and sneaky way to get kids to eat more fiber, here is a very simple recipe with a milder taste than most whole grains. Oat flour has more soluble fiber than whole wheat flour.

Makes three 1½-pound loaves. The recipe is easily doubled or halved.

3¼ cups lukewarm water
1½ tablespoons granulated yeast (1½ packets)
1½ tablespoons salt
1 cup oat flour
5½ cups unbleached all-purpose flour
Neutral-tasting oil for greasing the pan

1. **Mixing and storing the dough:** Mix the yeast and salt with the water in a 5-quart bowl, or a lidded (not airtight) food container.

2. Mix in the flours without kneading, using a spoon, a 14-cup capacity food processor (with dough attachment), or a heavy-duty stand mixer (with dough hook). If you're not using a machine, you may need to use wet hands to incorporate the last bit of flour.

3. Cover (not airtight), and allow to rest at room temperature until the dough rises and collapses (or flattens on top), approximately 2 hours.

4. The dough can be used immediately after the initial rise, though it is easier to handle when cold. Refrigerate in a lidded (not airtight) container and use over the next 10 days.

5. **On baking day,** lightly grease a 9×5×3-inch nonstick loaf pan. Dust the surface of the refrigerated dough with flour and cut off a 1½-pound (cantaloupe-size) piece. Dust the piece with more flour and quickly shape it into a ball by stretching the surface of the dough

around to the bottom on all four sides, rotating the ball a quarter-turn as you go. Drop into the prepared pan. Allow to rest and rise for 1 hour and 40 minutes (or just 40 minutes if you're using fresh, unrefrigerated dough).

6. **Twenty minutes before baking time, preheat the oven to 400°F,** with an empty broiler tray on any other shelf that won't interfere with the rising bread. The baking stone is not essential for loaf pan breads; if you omit it, the preheat may be as short as 5 minutes.

7. Place the loaf on a rack near the center of the oven. Pour 1 cup of hot tap water into the broiler tray and quickly close the oven door. Bake for 45 minutes, or until deeply browned and firm. Smaller or larger loaves will require adjustments in baking time.

8. Allow to cool before slicing or eating

Vermont Cheddar Bread

Great cheese bread is a wonderful American specialty, and a complete meal in a slice. The success of this loaf will depend on the cheese you use, so go with a great one.

"I grew up in Vermont, where eating sharp, aged cheddar is a birthright. Every Vermont bakery offers its own version of cheddar bread, using cheese from local dairies. We lived near Shelburne Farms, and I'm still loyal to their cheddar even since moving to the Midwest. It can be found at Whole Foods and other grocers with a good cheese counter. Feel free to substitute your favorite cheddar or other sharp-flavored hard cheese."—Zoë

Makes four 1-pound loaves. The recipe is easily doubled or halved.

3 cups lukewarm water
1½ tablespoons granulated yeast (1½ packets)
1½ tablespoons salt
1½ tablespoons sugar
6½ cups unbleached all-purpose flour
1 cup grated cheddar cheese

1. **Mixing and storing the dough:** Mix the yeast, salt, and sugar with the water in a 5-quart bowl, or a lidded (not airtight) food container.

2. Mix in the dry ingredients and the cheese without kneading, using a spoon, a 14-cup capacity food processor (with dough attachment), or a heavy-duty stand mixer (with dough hook). If you're not using a machine, you may need to use wet hands to incorporate the last bit of flour.

3. Cover (not airtight), and allow to rest at room temperature until the dough rises and collapses (or flattens on top), approximately 2 hours.

4. The dough can be used immediately after the initial rise, though it is easier to handle when cold. Refrigerate in a lidded (not airtight) container and use over the next 7 days.

5. **On baking day,** dust the surface of the refrigerated dough with flour and cut off a 1-pound (grapefruit-size) piece. Dust the piece with more flour and quickly shape it into a ball by stretching the surface of the dough around to the bottom on all four sides, rotating the ball a quarter-turn as you go. Allow to rest and rise on a cornmeal-covered pizza peel for 1 hour (or just 40 minutes if you're using fresh, unrefrigerated dough).

6. **Twenty minutes before baking time, preheat the oven to 450°F,** with a baking stone placed on the lowest rack. Place an empty broiler tray on any other shelf that won't interfere with the rising bread.

7. Sprinkle the loaf liberally with flour and slash a cross, "scallop," or tic-tac-toe pattern into the top, using a serrated bread knife (see photo, page 29). Leave the flour in place for baking; tap some of it off before eating.

8. Slide the loaf directly onto the hot stone. Pour 1 cup of hot tap water into the broiler tray, and quickly close the oven door. Bake for about 25 minutes, or until deeply browned and firm. Smaller or larger loaves will require adjustments in baking time.

9. Allow to cool before slicing or eating.

Caramelized Onion and Herb Dinner Rolls

"A friend once told me she times her cooking so that the onions are caramelizing as her guests arrive, claiming there is nothing more aromatic and inviting. I can't help but agree with her."—Zoë

Caramelizing the onions is easy and rewarding and can be used to dress up any of our savory doughs. Another favorite is to use the onion mixture with Manchego cheese as a pizza topping (page 137). Because it takes some time to achieve perfectly caramelized onions you may want to double the recipe to have some on hand; they freeze for months.

Makes 6 dinner rolls

Use any of these refrigerated pre-mixed doughs: Boule (page 26), Vermont Cheddar (page 106), or European Peasant (page 46)

1 pound (grapefruit-size portion) of any pre-mixed dough listed above
3 tablespoons olive oil
2 large onions, chopped
1 teaspoon salt
1 tablespoon vermouth or white wine
1 teaspoon white wine vinegar
2 tablespoons brown sugar
1 teaspoon dried thyme or oregano (or 2 teaspoons chopped fresh thyme and oregano leaves)
4 tablespoons water
Freshly ground black pepper to taste
Cornmeal for pizza peel

1. Heat the olive oil in a large skillet on medium-low heat. Add the onions, salt, vermouth, vinegar, brown sugar, herbs, and water to the oil and cook for about 25 minutes, stirring occasionally, until the onions are nicely caramelized. Add more water when needed to prevent burning.

2. Dust the surface of the refrigerated dough with flour and cut off a 1-pound (grapefruit-size) piece. Dust the piece with more flour and quickly shape it into a ball by stretching the surface of the dough around to the bottom on all four sides, rotating the ball a quarter-turn as you go.

3. To form the dinner rolls, divide the ball into 6 roughly equal portions (each about the size of a plum). Shape each one into a smooth ball. Allow them to rest and rise on a cornmeal-covered pizza peel for 40 minutes (or just 20 minutes if you're using fresh, unrefrigerated dough).

4. **Twenty minutes before baking time, preheat the oven to 450°F**, with a baking stone placed on the middle rack. Place an empty broiler tray on any other shelf that won't interfere with the rising bread.

5. Just before baking, sprinkle the rolls liberally with flour and cut a ½-inch cross pattern into the top, using a serrated bread knife or sharp kitchen scissors. Fill the resulting space with about 1 tablespoon of the onion mixture.

6. Slide the rolls directly onto the hot stone. Pour 1 cup of hot tap water into the broiler tray, and quickly close the oven door. Bake for 20 to 25 minutes, or until deeply browned and firm.

7. Allow to cool before eating.

Spinach Feta Bread

Spinach and feta cheese are usually seen wrapped in flaky phyllo pastry dough as savory Greek spinach pies. Our bread version is hearty, satisfying, and much easier to make. Serve with Greek olives for a fantastic and easy appetizer.

Makes four 1-pound loaves. The recipe is easily doubled or halved.

1 cup packed cooked (lightly steamed, boiled, or sautéed), chopped spinach
3 cups lukewarm water
1½ tablespoons granulated yeast (1½ packets)
1 tablespoon salt
⅔ cup crumbled feta cheese
1½ tablespoons sugar
6½ cups all-purpose flour
Cornmeal for pizza peel

1. **Mixing and storing the dough:** Squeeze the cooked spinach through a strainer to get rid of excess liquid.

2. Mix the yeast, salt, spinach, cheese, and sugar with the water in a 5-quart bowl, or a lidded (not airtight) food container.

3. Mix in the flour without kneading, using a spoon, a 14-cup capacity food processor (with dough attachment), or a heavy-duty stand mixer (with dough hook). If you're not using a machine, you may need to use wet hands to incorporate the last bit of flour.

4. Cover (not airtight), and allow to rest at room temperature until the dough rises and collapses (or flattens on top), approximately 2 hours.

5. The dough can be used immediately after the initial rise, though it is easier to handle when cold. Refrigerate in a lidded (not airtight) container and use over the next 7 days.

6. **On baking day,** dust the surface of the refrigerated dough with flour
   and cut off a 1-pound (grapefruit-size) piece. Dust the piece with
   more flour and quickly shape it into a ball by stretching the surface of
   the dough around to the bottom on all four sides, rotating the ball a
   quarter-turn as you go. Allow to rest and rise on a cornmeal-covered
   pizza peel for 1 hour (or just 40 minutes if you're using fresh,
   unrefrigerated dough).

7. **Twenty minutes before baking time, preheat the oven to 450°F,** with a
   baking stone placed on the middle rack. Place an empty broiler tray on
   any other shelf that won't interfere with the rising bread.

8. Sprinkle the loaf liberally with flour and slash a cross, "scallop," or tic-
   tac-toe pattern into the top, using a serrated bread knife (see photo,
   page 29). Leave the flour in place for baking; tap some of it off before
   eating.

9. Slide the loaf directly onto the hot stone. Pour 1 cup of hot tap water
   into the broiler tray, and quickly close the oven door. Bake for 30 to 35
   minutes, or until deeply browned and firm. Smaller or larger loaves
   will require adjustments in baking time.

10. Allow to cool before slicing or eating.

Sun-Dried Tomato and Parmesan Bread

Bright and intense tomato flavors harmonize nicely with the richness of aged Italian cheese. That's a combination we love in pasta dishes, so we created a bread with those flavors. If you can get authentic Parmigiano-Reggiano, use it here; if not, use whatever hard Italian-style grating cheese you like on your pasta.

Makes 1 loaf

Use any of these refrigerated pre-mixed doughs: Boule (page 26), European Peasant (page 46), Olive Oil (page 134), Light Whole Wheat (page 74), or Italian Semolina (page 80)
1 pound (grapefruit-size portion) of any pre-mixed dough listed above
Olive oil for brushing the loaf
½ cup oil-packed, sun-dried tomatoes, roughly chopped
½ cup grated Parmigiano-Reggiano cheese (or other Italian-style grating cheese)
Cornmeal for pizza peel

1. **On baking day,** dust the surface of the refrigerated dough with flour and cut off a 1-pound (grapefruit-size) piece. Dust the piece with more flour and quickly shape it into a ball by stretching the surface of the dough around to the bottom on all four sides, rotating the ball a quarter-turn as you go.

2. Roll out the ball into a ¼-inch-thick rectangle. As you roll out the dough, use enough flour to prevent it from sticking to the work surface but not so much as to make the dough dry.

3. Brush the dough with olive oil. Scatter the sun-dried tomatoes evenly over the dough and sprinkle the cheese over the tomatoes. Starting from the short end, roll the dough into a log and gently tuck the ends under to form an oval loaf. Allow to rest and rise on a cornmeal-covered

pizza peel for 1 hour (or just 40 minutes if you're using fresh, unrefrigerated dough).

4. **Twenty minutes before baking time, preheat the oven to 450°F,** with a baking stone placed on the middle rack. Place an empty broiler tray on any other shelf that won't interfere with the rising bread.

5. Brush the top of the dough lightly with olive oil and slash parallel cuts across the loaf, using a serrated bread knife.

6. Slide the loaf directly onto the hot stone. Pour 1 cup of hot tap water into the broiler tray, and quickly close the oven door. Bake for 30 to 35 minutes, or until deeply browned and firm.

7. Allow to cool before slicing or eating.

Aunt Melissa's Granola Bread

The key to great granola bread, is—surprise—great homemade granola (recipe follows). You can use packaged granola but it won't have quite the same flavor. Make lots of your own and there'll be plenty left over for breakfast.

"As a small child, I lived on a commune in the North East Kingdom of Vermont with my dad and my Aunt Melissa, where they made granola and bread to sell at the local co-op. My main contribution was to eat great quantities of the granola. I still remember the sweet earthy smell of the house when Melissa would bake. Aunt Melissa has since passed away, and with her went the original recipe, but this is a very close approximation."—Zoë

Makes two 1½-pound loaves. The recipe is easily doubled or halved.

2 cups lukewarm water
1½ tablespoons granulated yeast (1½ packets)
½ cup honey
1 tablespoon canola oil
1 teaspoon ground cinnamon
1 tablespoon salt
1½ cups whole wheat flour
2½ cups unbleached all-purpose flour
1½ cups granola, plus a few tablespoons to sprinkle on top (see page 116 for
    Homemade Granola)
Neutral-tasting oil for greasing the pan
Egg wash (1 egg beaten with 1 tablespoon of water)

1. **Mixing and storing the dough:** Mix the yeast, honey, canola oil, cinnamon, and salt with the water in a 5-quart bowl, or a lidded (not airtight) food container.

2. Mix in the flours and granola without kneading, using a spoon, a 14-cup capacity food processor (with dough attachment), or a heavy-duty

stand mixer (with dough hook). If you're not using a machine, you may need to use wet hands to incorporate the last bit of flour.

3. Cover (not airtight), and allow to rest at room temperature until the dough rises and collapses (or flattens on top), approximately 2 hours.

4. The dough can be used immediately after the initial rise, though it is easier to handle when cold. Refrigerate in a lidded (not airtight) container and use over the next 5 days.

5. **On baking day,** grease a 9×4×3-inch nonstick loaf pan. Dust the surface of the refrigerated dough with flour and cut off a 1½-pound (grapefruit-size) piece. Dust the piece with more flour and quickly shape it into a ball by stretching the surface of the dough around to the bottom on all four sides, rotating the ball a quarter-turn as you go. Drop into the prepared pan. Allow to rest and rise for 1 hour and 40 minutes (or just 1 hour if you're using fresh, unrefrigerated dough).

6. **Twenty minutes before baking time, preheat the oven to 375°F.**

7. Place the bread in the center of the oven and bake for about 45 minutes, or until richly browned and firm.

8. Allow to cool before slicing or eating.

Homemade Granola for Granola Bread

Use this granola in Aunt Melissa's Granola Bread, or enjoy it with milk for breakfast.

Makes about 6 cups

⅓ cup honey
¼ cup maple syrup
⅓ cup canola oil
2 tablespoons water
½ teaspoon vanilla extract
¼ teaspoon ground cinnamon
¼ teaspoon salt
4 cups rolled oats
¼ cup sesame seeds
¾ cup chopped pecans or the nut of your choice
¾ cup shredded unsweetened coconut
½ cup raisins
½ cup dried cherries, chopped dried apricots, or dried cranberries (or a
    combination)

1. **Preheat the oven to 350°F.** Prepare a high-sided cookie sheet or a lasagne pan with parchment paper, oil, butter, or a large silicone mat.

2. Mix honey, maple syrup, oil, water, vanilla extract, cinnamon, and salt in a large measuring cup.

3. In a large bowl, combine the liquid mixture with the dry ingredients, except for the dried fruit, and mix until everything is coated with the honey mixture. Spread the mixture evenly over the prepared baking sheet. Bake for about 30 minutes, stirring every 10 minutes, until the

granola is golden brown. Baking time will vary, depending on the depth of granola in the cookie sheet or pan.

4. After the baking is complete, add the dried fruit.

5. Allow to cool, store in jars, and use in Aunt Melissa's Granola Bread (page 114).

Roasted Garlic Potato Bread

Skin on and roughly mashed is the way we prefer our potatoes, but if you want yours peeled and perfectly pureed that will work as well. The roasted garlic is sweet and pungent; this bread explodes with aroma when you break into it.

Makes four 1-pound loaves. The recipe is easily doubled or halved.

1 whole head of garlic
3 cups lukewarm water
1½ tablespoons granulated yeast (1½ packets)
1½ tablespoons salt
1½ tablespoons sugar
1 cup mashed potato
6½ cups unbleached all-purpose flour
Cornmeal for pizza peel

1. Roast a whole head of garlic by wrapping it in aluminum foil and baking for 30 minutes at 400°F. Allow to cool and cut off the top of the head. Squeeze out the roasted garlic, measure 2 tablespoons, and set aside.

2. **Mixing and storing the dough:** Mix the yeast, salt, sugar, mashed potato, and reserved roasted garlic with the water in a 5-quart bowl, or a lidded (not airtight) food container.

3. Mix in the flour without kneading, using a spoon, a 14-cup capacity food processor (with dough attachment), or a heavy-duty stand mixer (with dough hook). If you're not using a machine, you may need to use wet hands to incorporate the last bit of flour.

4. Cover (not airtight), and allow to rest at room temperature until the dough rises and collapses (or flattens on top), approximately 2 hours.

5. The dough can be used immediately after the initial rise, though it is easier to handle when cold. Refrigerate in a lidded (not airtight) container and use over the next 7 days.

6. **On baking day,** dust the surface of the refrigerated dough with flour and cut off a 1-pound (grapefruit-size) piece. Dust the piece with more flour and quickly shape it into a ball by stretching the surface of the dough around to the bottom on all four sides, rotating the ball a quarter-turn as you go. Allow to rest and rise on a cornmeal-covered pizza peel for 1 hour (or just 40 minutes if you're using fresh, unrefrigerated dough).

7. **Twenty minutes before baking time, preheat the oven to 450°F,** with a baking stone placed on the middle rack of the oven. Place a broiler tray for water on any other shelf that won't interfere with the rising bread.

8. Sprinkle the loaf liberally with flour and slash a cross, "scallop," or tic-tac-toe pattern into the top, using a serrated bread knife (see photo, page 29). Leave the flour in place for baking; tap some of it off before eating.

9. Slide the loaf directly onto the hot stone. Pour 1 cup of hot tap water into the broiler tray, and quickly close the oven door. Bake for 30 to 35 minutes, or until deeply browned and firm. Smaller or larger loaves will require adjustments in baking time.

10. Allow to cool before slicing or eating.

Eastern European Potato-Rye Bread

Here's another potato bread, with a difference. Hold the roasted garlic and bring on the caraway seeds. This one's a very moist and rustic Eastern European masterpiece. The bread will still be fresh the day after baking because the potato and rye hold moisture and prevent it from drying out.

Makes four 1-pound loaves. The recipe is easily doubled or halved.

3 cups lukewarm water
1½ tablespoons granulated yeast (1½ packets)
1½ tablespoons salt
1 cup mashed potato
1½ tablespoons caraway seeds, plus additional for sprinkling on the top crust
1 cup rye flour
5½ cups unbleached all-purpose flour
Cornmeal for pizza peel
Cornstarch wash (see sidebar, page 51)

1. **Mixing and storing the dough:** Mix the yeast, salt, mashed potato, and caraway seeds with the water in a 5-quart bowl, or a lidded (not airtight) food container.

2. Mix in the rye and all-purpose flour without kneading, using a spoon, a 14-cup capacity food processor (with dough attachment), or a heavy-duty stand mixer (with dough hook). If you're not using a machine, you may need to use wet hands to incorporate the last bit of flour.

3. Cover (not airtight), and allow to rest at room temperature until the dough rises and collapses (or flattens on top), approximately 2 hours.

4. The dough can be used immediately after the initial rise, though it is easier to handle when cold. Refrigerate in a lidded (not airtight) container and use over the next 9 days.

5. **On baking day,** dust the surface of the refrigerated dough with flour and cut off a 1-pound (grapefruit-size) piece. Dust the piece with more flour and quickly shape it into a ball by stretching the surface of the dough around to the bottom on all four sides, rotating the ball a quarter-turn as you go. Allow to rest and rise on a cornmeal-covered pizza peel for 1 hour (or just 40 minutes if you're using fresh, unrefrigerated dough).

6. **Twenty minutes before baking time, preheat the oven to 450°F,** with a baking stone placed on the middle rack. Place an empty broiler tray on any other shelf that won't interfere with the rising bread.

7. Using a pastry brush, paint the top crust with cornstarch wash and then sprinkle with the additional caraway seeds. Slash the loaf with deep parallel cuts across the loaf; the cornstarch wash should allow the knife to pass without sticking.

8. Slide the loaf directly onto the hot stone. Pour 1 cup of hot tap water into the broiler tray, and quickly close the oven door. Bake for 30 to 35 minutes, until deeply browned and firm. Smaller or larger loaves will require adjustments in baking time.

9. Allow to cool before slicing or eating.

Bagels

These bagels are lighter than typical American-style bagels because we let them rest briefly while the oven is heating up, rather than boiling them immediately after shaping. They can be made the traditional way (forming and immediately boiling) for a denser result. This dough stores as well as any of our other recipes and can be used for soft pretzels (page 127), bialys (page 125), or even free-form loaves.

Makes about 20 bagels. The recipe is easily doubled or halved.

The Dough
3 cups lukewarm water
1½ tablespoons granulated yeast (1½ packets)
1½ tablespoons salt
1½ tablespoons sugar
6¼ cups bread flour

The Boiling-Pot
8 quarts boiling water
¼ cup sugar
1 teaspoon baking soda
Poppy or sesame seeds
Extra flour for dusting towel
Whole wheat flour for pizza peel

1. **Mixing and storing the bagel dough:** Mix the yeast, salt, and sugar with the water in a 5-quart bowl, or a lidded (not airtight) food container.

2. Mix in the flour without kneading, using a spoon, a 14-cup capacity food processor (with dough attachment), or a heavy-duty stand mixer (with dough hook). If you're not using a machine, you may need to use wet hands to incorporate the last bit of flour.

3. Cover (not airtight), and allow to rest at room temperature until the dough rises and collapses (or flattens on top), approximately 2 hours.

4. The dough can be used immediately after the initial rise, though it is easier to handle when cold. Refrigerate in a lidded (not airtight) container and use over the next 14 days.

Forming, Boiling, and Baking the Bagels

5. **Twenty minutes before baking time, preheat the oven to 400°F,** with a baking stone placed near the middle. Place an empty broiler tray on any other shelf that won't interfere with the rising bagels.

6. Dust the surface of the refrigerated dough with flour and cut off a 3-ounce piece of dough (about the size of a small peach). Dust the piece with more flour and quickly shape it into a ball by stretching the surface of the dough around to the bottom on all four sides, rotating the ball a quarter-turn as you go.

7. Repeat to form the rest of the bagels. Cover the balls loosely with plastic wrap and allow to rest at room temperature for 20 minutes.

8. **Prepare the boiling-pot:** Bring a large saucepan or stockpot full of water to a boil. Reduce to a simmer and add the sugar and baking soda.

9. Punch your thumb through the dough to form the hole. Ease it open with your fingers until the hole's diameter is about triple the width of the bagel wall (see photo, page 39).

10. Drop the bagels into the simmering water one at a time, making sure they are not crowding one another. They need enough room to float without touching or they will be misshapen. Let them simmer for 2

minutes and then flip them over with a slotted spoon to cook the other side. Simmer for another minute.

11. Remove them from the water, using the slotted spoon, and place on a clean kitchen towel that has been lightly dusted with flour. This will absorb some of the excess water from the bagels. Then place them on a peel covered with whole wheat flour. Sprinkle the bagels with poppy or sesame seeds.

12. Slide the bagels directly onto the hot stone. Pour 1 cup of hot tap water into the broiler tray, and quickly close the oven door. Bake with steam for about 20 minutes, until deeply browned and firm.

13. Break the usual rule for cooling, and serve these a bit warm—they're fantastic!

Bialys

"Bialys have always been something of an obsession for my mother. When I was a little girl, we'd visit my great aunts in Brighton Beach, Brooklyn, and my mother would always stop to pick up bialys and knishes, two things that couldn't be found anywhere in Vermont. Mom's obsession was in full bloom during a recent trip to New York City with her best friend, Barbara. As they left the ballet at Lincoln Center, my mother decided that late-night bialys would make the evening truly perfect. They jumped onto a bus and headed for Kossar's Bakery in lower Manhattan, one of the world's last great bastions of "bialydom." One can only imagine the sight of two women dressed for the ballet getting out of a bus at midnight in front of Kossar's. Only someone obsessed with fresh bialys would understand. Now my mother can make bialys at home."—Zoë

Makes about 5 bialys

1 pound Bagel dough (page 122)
1 tablespoon vegetable oil
½ onion, finely chopped
¾ teaspoon poppy seeds
Salt and pepper
Whole wheat flour for pizza peel

1. Dust the surface of the refrigerated dough with flour and cut off a 3-ounce piece of dough (about the size of a small peach). Dust the piece with more flour and quickly shape it into a ball by stretching the surface of the dough around to the bottom on all four sides, rotating the ball a quarter-turn as you go. Press the ball into a 3-inch disk and let rest on a floured surface for 30 minutes. Repeat with as many bialys as you want to bake.

2. **Twenty minutes before baking time, preheat the oven to 450°F,** with a baking stone placed near the middle of the oven. Place an empty broiler tray on any other shelf that won't interfere with the rising bialys.

3. While the dough is resting and the oven is preheating, sauté the onions in the vegetable oil over medium heat, until they are translucent and slightly golden. Don't overbrown at this stage, or they will burn in the oven. Remove from heat and add the poppy seeds, and salt and pepper to taste.

4. Press the center of each bialy to flatten it, working your way out until there is a ½-inch rim of dough that is not pressed flat and the bialy is about 4 inches wide. Fill the center with 1 tablespoon of the onion mixture and press it securely into the bialy dough.

5. Dust a pizza peel with whole wheat flour and put the finished bialys on it. Slide the bialys directly onto the hot stone, making sure they are spaced about an inch apart so they have room to expand. Pour 1 cup of hot tap water into the broiler tray, and quickly close the oven door. Bake for about 12 minutes, until golden brown. Don't overbake the bialys or they will lose their chewy soft texture.

6. Allow to cool slightly before eating.

Soft Pretzels

Pretzels are closely related to bagels, also having their origin in Central Europe. You can make fantastic pretzels using our basic Bagel dough (page 122), twisting it into the pretzel shape, which is a traditional symbol of earth and sun. We love them hot, with mustard.

"Food writer Mimi Sheraton ran a newspaper article on homemade pretzels about 30 years ago, and it stuck in my teenage mind—I was taken by her description of the crusty pretzels baked for her by her Stuttgart hosts. I still have the original clipping from 1978, so we've adapted her recipe here."—Jeff

Makes about 5 pretzels

The Dough
1 pound Bagel dough (page 122)
Egg wash (1 egg beaten with 1 tablespoon of water)
Coarse salt for sprinkling
Extra flour for dusting kitchen towel
Whole wheat flour for pizza peel

The Boiling-Pot
8 quarts boiling water
1 teaspoon baking soda
1 tablespoon cream of tartar

1. Dust the surface of the refrigerated dough with flour and cut off a 3-ounce piece of dough (about the size of a small peach). Dust the piece with more flour and quickly shape it into a ball by stretching the surface of the dough around to the bottom on all four sides, rotating the ball a quarter-turn as you go. Elongate the ball, dusting with additional flour as necessary. Roll it back and forth with your hands on a flour-dusted surface to form a long rope approximately ½ inch in diameter and 12 inches long.

2. Twist into a pretzel shape by first tying a knot, then looping the ends around and joining them back to the loop. Repeat, forming as many pretzels as you want to bake.

3. **Twenty minutes before baking time, preheat the oven to 450°F,** with a baking stone placed near the middle of the oven. Place an empty broiler tray on any other shelf that won't interfere with the rising pretzels.

4. Keep the pretzels covered loosely with plastic wrap as you repeat the process to make the rest. Let the pretzels rest at room temperature for 20 minutes.

5. **Prepare the boiling-pot:** Bring a large saucepan or stockpot full of water to a boil. Reduce to a simmer and add the baking soda and cream of tartar. Drop the pretzels into the simmering water one at a time, making sure they are not crowding one another. They need enough room to float without touching or they will be misshapen. Let them simmer for 2 minutes and then flip them over with a slotted spoon to cook the other side. Simmer for another minute.

6. Remove them from the water, using the slotted spoon, and place on a clean kitchen towel that has been lightly dusted with flour. This will absorb some of the excess water from the pretzels. Then place them on a peel covered with whole wheat flour. Brush with egg wash and sprinkle with coarse salt.

7. Slide the pretzels directly onto the hot stone. Pour 1 cup of hot tap water into the broiler tray, and quickly close the oven door. Bake with steam for about 15 minutes, until deeply browned and firm. If you want crisp pretzels, bake 5 to 10 minutes longer.

8. Serve these a bit warm, with a hefty stein of beer.

Montreal Bagels

These differ from American-style bagels by the addition of malt powder and honey, and the fact that the toppings are on both sides. In Montreal, bagels are traditionally baked in a wood-fired oven, which imparts a wonderful smokiness, but the ones made on the baking stone at home are excellent as well. This recipe calls for bread flour to ensure that the bagels are nice and chewy—all-purpose flour makes them too cakey.

"My husband, Graham, grew up in Canada eating Montreal bagels. One of the first things we did as a couple was to visit Montreal. As soon as we arrived, we drove to Fairmont Bagels and got a bag of fresh hot bagels— I was in love. Several years later, after a New Year's Eve party in Montreal, Graham proposed to me while eating our favorite bagels. Now that we live in the Midwest without our beloved bagels, I create my own. They may not be baked in a wood-fired oven but they are close, really close, to what I remember."—Zoë

Makes about 1 dozen bagels. The recipe is easily doubled or halved.

The Dough
1½ cups lukewarm water
1 tablespoon granulated yeast (1½ packets)
2 teaspoons salt
5 tablespoons sugar
2 tablespoons honey
1 egg
3 tablespoons canola oil
3 tablespoons malt powder
4¼ cups bread flour
Poppy or sesame seeds
Whole wheat flour for pizza peel

The Boiling-Pot
4 quarts of water
2 tablespoons honey
2 tablespoons malt powder

1. **Mixing and storing the bagel dough:** Mix the yeast, salt, sugar, honey, egg, oil, and malt powder with the lukewarm water in a 5-quart bowl, or a lidded (not airtight) food container.

2. Mix in the flour without kneading, using a spoon, a 14-cup capacity food processor (with dough attachment), or a heavy-duty stand mixer (with dough hook). If you're not using a machine, you may need to use wet hands to incorporate the last bit of flour.

3. Cover (not airtight), and allow to rest at room temperature until the dough rises and collapses (or flattens on top), approximately 2 hours.

4. The dough can be used immediately after the initial rise, though it is easier to handle when cold. Refrigerate in a lidded (not airtight) container and use over the next 10 days.

Forming, Boiling, and Baking the Bagels

5. **Preheat the oven to 400°F,** with a baking stone near the middle of the oven. Place an empty broiler tray on any other shelf that won't interfere with the rising bagels.

6. Dust the surface of the refrigerated dough with flour and cut off a 3-ounce piece of dough (about the size of a small peach). Dust with more flour and quickly shape it into a ball by stretching the surface of the dough around to the bottom on all four sides, rotating the ball a quarter-turn as you go.

7. Repeat to form the rest of the bagels. Cover the balls loosely with plastic wrap and allow to rest at room temperature for 20 minutes.

8. **Prepare the boiling-pot:** Bring a large saucepan or stockpot full of water to a boil. Reduce to a simmer and add the honey and malt powder.

9. Punch your thumb through the dough to form the hole. Ease it open with your fingers until the hole's diameter is about triple the width of the bagel wall (see photo, page 39).

10. Drop the bagels into the water one at a time, making sure they are not crowding each other. They need enough room to float without touching or they will be misshapen. Let them simmer for 1 minute and then flip them over with a slotted spoon and cook the other side for 30 seconds.

11. Remove them from the water, using the slotted spoon, and place on a clean kitchen towel that has been lightly dusted with flour. This will absorb some of the excess water from the bagels.

12. Dredge each bagel in poppy or sesame seeds *on both sides* and place on a pizza peel. If making plain bagels, cover the peel with whole wheat flour. Slide the bagels directly onto the hot stone. Pour 1 cup of hot tap water into the broiler tray, and quickly close the oven door. Bake with steam for about 20 minutes, until richly browned and firm.

13. Break the usual rule for cooling and serve these a bit warm.

7

FLATBREADS AND PIZZAS

Flatbreads from Southern Europe (Italian *focaccia*, French Provençal *fougasse*) have been popular in the U.S. for years (though not as long as pizza). When they first arrived on the scene, their strong flavors seemed exotic, with their luxurious richness and weight derived from olive oil rather than milk, butter, or cream. But their originators would have laughed; these were simple peasant loaves, everyday fare without pretension. These fragrant rounds were born in regions where dairy and butter were greater luxuries than olive oil.

And the Middle East has been producing leavened but flat breads of all kinds for thousands of years. Most Americans are familiar with puffed pita flatbread, but the aromatic spice-topped Arab *za'atar* flatbread is uncommon outside the Middle East.

Flatbread is marvelously suited to very fast preparation. Because flatbreads are so thin, the dough will warm to room temperature quickly, which means very short, if any, rise time. Pizza, *lavash*, and pita, among others, need none. And thicker flatbreads like focaccia do very well with just 15 to 20 minutes, so preheat the oven while you're shaping them.

Once they've had their brief rest, flatbreads also bake faster, as quickly as five minutes for *lavash* and pita (pages 168 and 163). So if you've stored some dough, you can have fresh flatbread on the table in about 25 minutes!

Olive Oil Dough

This versatile, rich dough works nicely in pizza, *focaccia*, or olive bread. The fruitier the olive oil, the better the flavor.

Makes four 1-pound loaves. The recipe is easily doubled or halved.

2¾ cups lukewarm water
1½ tablespoons granulated yeast (1½ packets)
1½ tablespoons salt
1 tablespoon sugar
¼ cup extra virgin olive oil
6½ cups unbleached all-purpose flour

1. Mix the yeast, salt, sugar, and olive oil with the water in a 5-quart bowl, or a lidded (not airtight) food container.

2. Mix in the flour without kneading, using a spoon, a 14-cup capacity food processor (with dough attachment), or a heavy-duty stand mixer (with dough hook). If you're not using a machine, you may need to use wet hands to incorporate the last bit of flour.

3. Cover (not airtight), and allow to rest at room temperature until dough rises and collapses (or flattens on top), approximately 2 hours.

4. The dough can be used immediately after the initial rise, though it is easier to handle when cold. Refrigerate in a lidded (not airtight) container and use over the next 12 days.

Neapolitan Pizza with Eggplant and Anchovy

No one ever seems to tire of pizza, so here's our version. We like crisp, thin-crusted, Neapolitan-style pizza, baked at a very high temperature directly on the stone. In home ovens, the maximum temperature is 500°F or 550°F—not 700°F as in Naples! Pizza made this way at home, especially if you can get fresh mozzarella, is unlike anything most of us are used to eating. The secret to Neapolitan pizza is to keep the crust thin, don't overload it with toppings, and bake it very quickly at a high temperature so it doesn't all cook down to a soup. You should be able to appreciate the individual ingredients in the topping when the pizza emerges from the oven. And of course, you can put any toppings you like on this pizza.

Makes 1 medium-size pizza (12 to 14 inches) to serve 2 to 4

Use any of these refrigerated pre-mixed doughs: Boule (page 26), European Peasant (page 46), Olive Oil (page 134), Light Whole Wheat (page 74), or Italian Semolina (page 80)
1 pound (grapefruit-size portion) of any pre-mixed dough listed above
½ cup canned Italian-style chopped tomatoes, strained and pressed of liquid (or substitute prepared tomato sauce)
½ small eggplant, sliced into ⅛-inch-thick rounds, cut into bite-size pieces, and brushed with olive oil
4 canned or jarred anchovy fillets, chopped
¼ pound sliced fresh mozzarella cheese, preferably buffalo-milk variety
1 tablespoon grated Parmigiano-Reggiano cheese
Cornmeal for covering the pizza peel

1. **Twenty minutes before baking time, preheat the oven with a baking stone at 550°F (or 500°F if that's your oven's maximum).** Shelf placement is not critical for pizza, and you won't be using steam, so you can omit the broiler tray.

2. Prepare and measure all the toppings in advance. The key to a pizza

that slides right off the peel is to work quickly—don't let the dough sit on the peel any longer than neccesary.

3. Dust the surface of the refrigerated dough with flour and cut off a 1-pound (grapefruit-size) piece. Dust the piece with more flour and quickly shape it into a ball by stretching the surface of the dough around to the bottom on all four sides, rotating the ball a quarter-turn as you go.

4. Flatten the dough with your hands and a rolling pin on a wooden board to produce a 1/8-inch-thick round, dust with flour to keep the dough from sticking to the rolling pin and board. A little sticking to the board can be helpful in overcoming the dough's resistance to stretch, so don't overuse flour, and consider using a dough scraper to "unstick" the dough from the board. You may also need to let the partially rolled dough sit for a few minutes to "relax" to allow further rolling. At this point, stretching by hand may help, followed by additional rolling. Place the rolled-out dough onto a liberally cornmeal-covered pizza peel.

5. Distribute the tomatoes over the surface of the dough. Do not cover the dough thickly; the quantity specified will leave some of the dough surface exposed.

6. Scatter the mozzarella over the surface of the dough, then the eggplant, anchovies, and Parmigiano-Reggiano. No further resting is needed prior to baking.

7. If you have an exhaust fan, turn it on now, because some of the cornmeal on the pizza peel will smoke at this temperature (see sidebar, page 137). Slide the pizza directly onto the stone (it may take a number of back-and-forth shakes to dislodge the pizza). Check for doneness in 8 to 10 minutes; at this time, turn the pizza around in the oven if one side is browning faster than the other. It may need up to 5 more minutes in the oven.

8. Allow to cool slightly on a cooling rack before serving, to allow the cheese to set.

VARIATIONS

Pizza Margherita: This is the classic Italian pizza, with nothing but mozzarella, tomato, and a sprinkling of dried oregano. Drizzle with extra-virgin olive oil just before baking for authenticity and flavor. If you have fresh oregano, coarsely chop the leaves and put them on the pizza first. Tomato sauce from a jar makes a quick substitute for canned tomatoes. On the other end of the spectrum, try the recipe with in-season fresh tomatoes, drained of seeds and liquid and thinly sliced.

Sausage or Pepperoni Pizza: Layer sliced cooked sausage or pepperoni on top of the cheese in a basic tomato and cheese pizza. Always use precooked sausage or the meat will render too much fat as the pizza bakes, which will make the pizza soggy.

Caramelized Onion and Manchego Cheese Pizza: This is a sophisticated combination of flavors, both sweet and savory. Use 1 cup of caramelized onions (page 108) covered with ¾ cup of grated Manchego cheese.

Don't Get Smoked Out of House and Home: This recipe calls for an exhaust fan because there'll be a lot of smoke from stray cornmeal on such a hot stone. Make sure the stone is scraped clean before preheating. If you don't have an exhaust fan, choose a lower oven temperature (450°F), and bake about 15 to 20 percent longer. Another option is to bake the pizza on an outdoor gas grill (see Gas Grill Flatbread Baking, pages 140–41).

Rustic Wild Mushroom and Potato Pizza Provençal

Herbes de Provence give this rustic creation of Zoë's a luscious flavor that will transport you to the lavender and thyme-scented hillsides of the south of France.

Makes 1 medium-size pizza (12 to 14 inches) to serve 2 to 4

Use any of these refrigerated pre-mixed doughs: Boule (page 26), European Peasant (page 46), Olive Oil (page 134), Light Whole Wheat (page 74), or Italian Semolina (page 80)

1 pound (grapefruit-size portion) of any pre-mixed dough listed above

2 small red new potatoes, skin on and thinly sliced

6 large wild mushrooms such as chanterelles, shiitakes, porcini, portobellos, or oyster mushrooms, *or* white mushrooms if wild are not available, thinly sliced

2 tablespoons olive oil

1 teaspoon *herbes de Provence*

Salt and freshly ground black pepper to taste

5 oil-packed sun-dried tomatoes, thinly sliced

2 ounces finely grated Parmigiano-Reggiano cheese

Cornmeal for covering the pizza peel

1. **Preheat a baking stone in the oven for at least 20 minutes at 550°F (or 500°F if that's your oven's maximum).** Shelf placement is not critical for pizza, and you won't be using steam, so you can omit the broiler tray.

2. Prepare and measure all the toppings in advance. The key to a pizza that slides right off the peel is to work quickly—don't let the dough sit on the peel any longer than necessary.

3. Sauté the potatoes and mushrooms in the olive oil until the potatoes are soft. Season with the *herbes de Provence*, salt, and pepper.

4. Dust the surface of the refrigerated dough with flour and cut off a 1-pound (grapefruit-size) piece. Dust the piece with more flour and quickly shape it into a ball by stretching the surface of the dough around to the bottom on all four sides, rotating the ball a quarter-turn as you go.

5. Flatten the dough with your hands and a rolling pin on a wooden board to produce a ⅛-inch-thick round. Dust with flour to keep the dough from sticking to the rolling pin and board. A little sticking to the board can be helpful in overcoming the dough's resistance to stretch, so don't overuse flour, and consider using a dough scraper to "unstick" the dough from the board. You may also need to let the partially rolled dough sit for a few minutes to "relax" and to allow further rolling. At this point, stretching by hand may help, followed by additional rolling. Place the rolled-out dough onto a liberally cornmeal-covered pizza peel.

> ◌◌
>
> **Don't Get Smoked Out of House and Home:** This recipe calls for an exhaust fan because there'll be a lot of smoke from stray cornmeal on such a hot stone. Make sure the stone is scraped clean before preheating. If you don't have an exhaust fan, choose a lower oven temperature (450°F), and bake about 15 to 20 percent longer. Another option is to bake the pizza on an outdoor gas grill (see Gas Grill Flatbread Baking, pages 140–41).

6. Distribute the potatoes, mushrooms, and sun-dried tomatoes over the surface of the dough. Do not cover the dough thickly; the quantity specified will leave some of the dough surface exposed.

7. Sprinkle the cheese over the surface of the dough.

8. If you have an exhaust fan, turn it on now, because some of the

cornmeal on the pizza peel will smoke at this temperature (see sidebar, previous page). Slide the pizza directly onto the stone (it may take a number of back-and-forth shakes to dislodge the pizza). Check for doneness in 8 to 10 minutes; at this time, turn the pizza around in the oven if one side is browning faster than the other. It may need up to 5 more minutes in the oven.

9. Allow to cool slightly on a cooling rack before serving, to allow the cheese to set.

Gas Grill Flatbread Baking

For those hot summer days when you want fresh bread but can't stand the idea of turning on the oven, outdoor gas grills are the answer. Gas grills with a thermometer and a baking stone can produce wonderful breads. When baking in a grill, thinner is better. Flatbreads like pita, naan, *lavash*, *focaccia*, and *fougasse* work wonderfully.

General Procedure for Gas Grill Baking:

1. Dust the surface of refrigerated flatbread dough with flour and cut off a 1-pound (grapefruit-size piece). Dust the piece with more flour and quickly shape it into a ball by stretching the surface of the dough around to the bottom on all four sides, rotating the ball a quarter-turn as you go. Form a flattened round loaf or a flatbread from your favorite recipe. Allow to rest and rise on a pizza peel as specified in the recipe.

2. **Twenty minutes before baking time**, place a baking stone on the gas grill. Light the grill and manipulate the burner controls to maintain desired temperature as

measured by the grill's thermometer. If the recipe calls for baking with steam, place a steel cup or pan on the stone, off to one side so as not to interfere with the baking bread. If your grill has a second shelf on which you can safely balance a broiler tray, use that for steam.

3. Slide the loaf onto the hot stone. Bake for about two-thirds of the recommended time, with steam if that's in the recipe.

4. Using a long-handed spatula, flip the bread over onto its top crust (even if this is pita bread). Remove the water receptacle if you used one.

5. Continue baking for the last one-third of the baking time, until the crust is firm and browned. If you're making pita, don't allow much browning.

Spinach and Cheese Calzone

Traditional pizzerias turn out folded cheese pies by using the basic ingredients that appear in pizza. We recommend whole-milk ricotta for a rich and creamy filling. The doubled dough thickness means that you need to bake at a lower oven temperature than used for the flat Neapolitan pizza.

Makes 1 medium-size calzone to serve 2 to 4

Use any of these refrigerated pre-mixed doughs: Boule (page 26), European Peasant (page 46), Olive Oil (page 134), Light Whole Wheat (page 74), or Italian Semolina (page 80)
1 pound (grapefruit-size portion) of any pre-mixed dough listed above
1 large garlic clove, minced
1 to 2 tablespoons olive oil
½ cup fresh or thawed and drained frozen spinach leaves
1 egg
1 cup whole-milk ricotta cheese
¼ teaspoon salt
Freshly ground black pepper, to taste
Whole wheat flour for the pizza peel

1. **Twenty minutes before baking time, preheat the oven to 450°F,** with a baking stone. Place an empty broiler tray on any other shelf that won't interfere with the calzone as it rises.

2. Briefly sauté the garlic in the olive oil until fragrant. Add the spinach and sauté for 2 minutes, until wilted. Drain and squeeze the spinach gently, discarding any liquid that may have accumulated.

3. Beat the egg and blend with the ricotta cheese, salt, and pepper in a bowl. Mix the spinach with the cheese.

4. Dust the surface of the refrigerated dough with flour and cut off a 1-

pound (grapefruit-size) piece. Dust the piece with more flour and quickly shape it into a ball by stretching the surface of the dough around to the bottom on all four sides, rotating the ball a quarter-turn as you go.

5. Flatten the dough with your hands and a rolling pin on a wooden board to produce a ⅛-inch-thick round, dusting lightly with flour, as needed, to keep the dough from sticking to the rolling pin and board. A little sticking to the board can be helpful in overcoming the dough's resistance to stretch, so don't overuse flour, and consider using a dough scraper to "unstick" dough from the board. You may also need to let the partially rolled dough sit for a few minutes to "relax" and allow for further rolling. At this point, hand-stretching may also help, followed by additional rolling. Place the rolled-out dough onto a pizza peel liberally covered with whole wheat flour.

6. Cover half the dough round with the cheese-spinach mixture, leaving a 1-inch border at the edge. Using a pastry brush, wet the border with water. Fold the bare side of the dough over the cheese mixture and seal the border by pinching closed with your fingers. Cut three slits in the top crust, all the way through the dough, using a serrated knife. No resting time is needed.

7. Slide the calzone directly onto the hot stone. Pour 1 cup of hot tap water into the broiler tray, and quickly close the oven door. Bake for about 25 minutes, or until golden brown.

8. Allow to cool for 10 minutes before serving to allow the cheese to set a bit.

Philadelphia Stromboli with Sausage

Both of us lived briefly in Philadelphia and fondly remember this local specialty. It's really just a folded pizza made with tomatoes, sausage, and mozzarella. It was brought to the table still puffed from the oven and glistening with olive oil. Unlike calzone (page 142) or red pepper *fougasse* (page 154), this is a flatbread that is meant to puff exuberantly, like pita bread, so don't slit the top crust prior to baking.

Makes 1 medium-size stromboli to serve 2 to 4

Use any of these refrigerated pre-mixed doughs: Boule (page 26), European Peasant (page 46), Olive Oil (page 134), Light Whole Wheat (page 74), or Italian Semolina (page 80)

1 pound (grapefruit-size portion) of any pre-mixed dough listed above

½ cup canned Italian-style chopped tomatoes, well-drained

1 sweet or hot Italian sausage, grilled and cut into ⅛-inch-thick slices

10 basil leaves, torn or cut into thin ribbons

½ pound sliced fresh mozzarella cheese, preferably buffalo-milk variety

Extra virgin olive oil, for brushing on top

Whole wheat flour for the pizza peel

1. **Twenty minutes before baking, preheat the oven to 450°F,** with a baking stone set near the middle of the oven. Place an empty broiler tray on any other shelf that won't interfere with the rising stromboli.

2. Dust the surface of the refrigerated dough with flour and cut off a 1-pound (grapefruit-size) piece. Dust the piece with more flour and quickly shape it into a ball by stretching the surface of the dough around to the bottom on all four sides, rotating the ball a quarter-turn as you go.

3. Flatten the dough with your hands and a rolling pin on a wooden board to produce a ⅛-inch-thick round, dusting lightly with flour, as

needed, to keep the dough from sticking to the rolling pin and board. A little sticking to the board can be helpful in overcoming the dough's resistance to stretch, so don't overuse flour, and consider using a dough scraper to "unstick" dough from the board. You may also need to let the partially rolled dough sit for a few minutes to "relax" and allow for further rolling. At this point, hand-stretching may also help, followed by additional rolling. Place the rolled-out dough onto a pizza peel, liberally covered with whole wheat flour.

4. Cover half the dough round with the tomato, sausage, basil, and then the cheese, leaving a 1-inch border at the edge.

5. Using a pastry brush, wet the border with water. Fold the bare side of dough over the cheese and seal the border by pinching closed with your fingers. Do not slit or slash the dough; *stromboli* is meant to puff. Brush the top crust with olive oil. No resting or rising time is needed

6. Slide the *stromboli* directly onto the hot stone. Pour 1 cup of hot tap water into the broiler tray, and quickly close the oven door. Bake for about 25 minutes, or until golden brown.

7. Allow to cool for 10 minutes before serving.

Prosciutto and Olive Oil Flatbread

"My friend Ralph's mother comes from Naples, and she remembers a bread from her childhood that was studded with pieces of pork fatback. The lardo *from the pork melted into the bread and created a fantastic rich crumb. The bread was called* pane di lardo.

"Since your local supermarket isn't likely to carry Italian-style pork fatback, we decided to try a more universally loved Italian meat. Prosciutto is a some-what expensive, aged, Italian ham, but there are reasonable domestic versions available as well. Spanish serrano *ham is close to prosciutto in style, and can also be used. The meat lends an incredible combination of sweet and savory that's nicely complemented by the rosemary. Serve this with chilled Prosecco, a sweet Italian sparkling wine, for a sublime appetizer."*—Jeff

Makes 6 appetizer portions

1 pound (grapefruit-size portion) Olive Oil dough (page 134)
¼ teaspoon dried rosemary, crumbled, or ½ teaspoon fresh
2 ounces (⅛ pound) sliced prosciutto or serrano ham, cut into 1-inch squares
Extra virgin olive oil, for brushing on top

1. Dust the surface of the refrigerated dough with flour and cut off a 1-pound (grapefruit-size) piece. Dust the piece with more flour and quickly shape it into a ball by stretching the surface of the dough around to the bottom on all four sides, rotating the ball a quarter-turn as you go. Using your hands and a rolling pin, flatten it to a thickness of about ½ inch.

2. Layer the meat onto the dough round and sprinkle it with the crumbled rosemary. Roll up the dough and shape into a ball. Flatten the ball to a thickness of approximately 1 inch, and allow to rest and rise on a cornmeal-covered pizza peel for 40 minutes (or just 20 minutes if you're using fresh, unrefrigerated dough).

Pain d'Epi and Couronne

Pumpernickel and Deli-Style Rye

Olive Bread, Roasted Red Pepper Fougasse, and Italian Semolina Bread

Neapolitan Pizza with Eggplant and Anchovy

Pita Bread

Brioche à Tête

Sunny-Side-Up Apricot Pastry

Pecan Caramel Rolls

3. **Twenty minutes before baking time, preheat the oven to 400°F,** with a baking stone placed near the middle of the oven. Place an empty broiler tray on any other shelf that won't interfere with the rising bread.

4. Just before baking, brush with cornstarch wash and slash a cross, "scallop," or tic-tac-toe pattern into the top, using a serrated bread knife (see photo, page 29).

5. Slide the loaf directly onto the hot stone. Pour 1 cup of hot tap water into the broiler tray, and quickly close the oven door. Bake for about 25 minutes, or until richly browned and firm.

6. Allow to cool before cutting into wedges and eating.

Pissaladière

When Julia Child revealed that much of the French repertoire could be mastered by casual home chefs in *Mastering the Art of French Cooking* (1961), she included a delightful recipe for *Pissaladière Niçoise*, an onion tart with anchovies and black olives in a rich pastry shell. As served in the south of France, this dish is often based on a rustic flatbread or pizza base rather than a pastry shell, so we adapted Julia's recipe for our approach. The original called for dry black Niçoise-style olives but we've found we like it just as well with black olives done in the wetter, Greek Kalamata style. We like fresh, bulk-sold olives, but use whatever you like. Pre-pitted olives have a bit less flavor but they're a timesaver. This makes a great summertime hors d'oeuvre, served with dry white wine.

Makes 6 appetizer portions

Use any of these refrigerated pre-mixed doughs: Boule (page 29), European Peasant (page 46), Olive Oil (page 134), Light Whole Wheat (page 74), or Italian Semolina (page 80)

1 pound (grapefruit-size portion) of any pre-mixed dough listed above

3 medium onions, minced

4 tablespoons olive oil

4 parsley sprigs, chopped

¼ teaspoon dried thyme, or ½ teaspoon fresh

½ bay leaf

2 large garlic cloves, chopped

½ teaspoon salt

Freshly ground pepper to taste

8 canned or jarred anchovy fillets, chopped

16 pitted Niçoise or Kalamata olives, halved

1. **Twenty minutes before baking time, preheat the oven with a baking stone at 550°F (500°F if that's the highest your oven goes).** Shelf placement is not critical, and you don't need a broiler tray since you won't be using steam.

2.   Sauté the onions in olive oil with the herbs, garlic, salt, and pepper over medium-low heat until barely browned, about 30 minutes. Don't over-brown, or they will burn while baking.

3.   Dust the surface of the refrigerated dough with flour and cut off a 1-pound (grapefruit-size) piece. Dust the piece with more flour and quickly shape it into a ball by stretching the surface of the dough around to the bottom on all four sides, rotating the ball a quarter-turn as you go.

4.   Flatten the dough with your hands and a rolling pin on a clean surface to produce a ⅛-inch-thick round, dusting lightly with flour, as needed, to keep the dough from sticking to the rolling pin and board. A little sticking to the board can be helpful in overcoming the dough's resistance to stretch, so don't overuse flour and consider using a dough scraper to "unstick" dough from the board. You may also need to let the partially rolled dough sit for a few minutes to "relax" and allow for further rolling. At this point, hand-stretching may also help, followed by additional rolling. Place the rolled-out dough onto a pizza peel liberally covered with cornmeal.

5.   Remove the bay leaf and spread the onion mixture and its oil over the dough. Scatter the anchovies and olives on top. If you have an exhaust fan, turn it on now, because some of the cornmeal will burn at this temperature (see sidebar, page 139).

6.   Slide the *pissaladière* directly onto the hot stone; it may take a number of back-and-forth shakes to dislodge it. Check for browning in 8 to 10 minutes. At this time you may have to turn the *pissaladière* around to achieve even doneness. It may need up to 5 more minutes in the oven.

7.   Cool slightly, cut into wedges or squares, and serve.

Focaccia with Onion and Rosemary

Here's the ultimate Tuscan hors d'oeuvre, with onion and rosemary topping on an olive oil dough. Try it with something simple, like rustic antipasto, or as an accompaniment to soups or pastas.

We bake onion *focaccia* at a slightly lower temperature than usual to avoid burning the onions, and we bake it on a cookie sheet rather than a baking stone since the oil absorbs into the stone and creates an annoying problem with kitchen smoke that can continue into the next several baking sessions.

The key to success with this recipe is to go light on the onion. If you completely cover the dough surface with onions, the *focaccia* just won't brown and the result, though delicious, will be pale.

Makes 6 appetizer portions

Use any of these refrigerated pre-mixed doughs: Olive Oil dough is our first choice (page 134), but you can also use Boule (page 26), European Peasant (page 46), Light Whole Wheat (page 74), or Italian Semolina (page 80)

Olive oil for greasing the cookie sheet

1 pound (grapefruit-size portion) of any pre-mixed dough listed above

¼ medium white or yellow onion, thinly sliced

2 tablespoons extra virgin olive oil, plus 1 teaspoon for drizzling

¾ teaspoon dried rosemary leaves (or 1½ teaspoons fresh)

Coarse salt and freshly ground pepper for sprinkling on top

1. **Twenty minutes before baking, preheat the oven to 425°F**, with an empty broiler tray on any shelf that won't interfere with the *focaccia*. The baking stone is not essential when using a cookie sheet; if you omit the stone the preheat can be as short as 5 minutes.

2. Grease a cookie sheet with a bit of olive oil or line with parchment paper or a silicone mat. Set aside. Dust the surface of the refrigerated dough with flour and cut off a 1-pound (grapefruit-size) piece. Dust the piece with more flour and quickly shape it into a ball by stretching

the surface of the dough around to the bottom on all four sides, rotating the ball a quarter-turn as you go.

3. Flatten it into a ½- to ¾-inch-thick round, using your hands and/or a rolling pin and a minimal amount of flour. Place the round on the prepared cookie sheet.

4. Sauté the onion slices in the 2 tablespoons of olive oil until softened but not browned; if you brown them they'll burn in the oven. Strew the onion sparingly over the surface of the dough, leaving a 1-inch border at the edge. Allow the majority of the dough surface to show through the onions as bare dough. (You may have leftover onion at the end.) If you can't see most of the dough surface, you're using too much onion and your *focaccia* won't brown attractively.

5. Sprinkle with rosemary, coarse salt, and freshly ground pepper. Finish with a light drizzle of the remaining olive oil over the surface, about 1 teaspoon, but not so much that it starts dripping off the sides. (As with the onion, you won't cover the whole surface with oil.)

6. Allow the *focaccia* to rest and rise for 20 minutes.

7. After the *focaccia* has rested, place the cookie sheet on a rack near the center of the oven. Pour 1 cup of hot tap water into the broiler tray and quickly close the oven door. Bake for about 25 minutes, or until the crust is medium brown. Be careful not to burn the onions. The baking time will vary according to the *focaccia*'s thickness. *Focaccia* will not develop a crackling crust, because of the olive oil.

8. Cut into wedges and serve warm.

Olive Fougasse

Provençal *fougasse* and Italian *focaccia* share a linguistic and culinary background. It's said that both may have Ancient Greek or Etruscan roots. *Fougasse* distinguishes itself with artful cutouts that resemble a leaf or ladder; this delivers a crusty result, with lots more surface exposed to the oven heat. As with *focaccia*, it's best to bake it on a cookie sheet to prevent oil from being absorbed into your baking stone. The halved olives infuse the dough with their essence.

Makes 6 appetizer portions

Use any of these refrigerated pre-mixed doughs: Olive Oil (page 134), Boule (page 26), European Peasant (page 46), Light Whole Wheat (page 74), or Italian Semolina (page 80)

1 pound (grapefruit-size portion) of any pre-mixed dough listed above

½ cup high-quality black olives, preferably Niçoise or Kalamata, pitted and halved or quartered if large

Olive oil for greasing the cookie sheet and brushing the *fougasse*

1. **Twenty minutes before baking time, preheat the oven to 400°F.** Place an empty broiler tray on any other shelf that won't interfere with rising bread. Grease a cookie sheet with a bit of olive oil. Set aside. The baking stone is not essential for breads made on a cookie sheet; if you omit it the preheat can be as short as 5 minutes.

2. Dust the surface of the refrigerated dough with flour and cut off a 1-pound (grapefruit-size) piece. Dust the piece with more flour and quickly shape it into a ball by stretching the surface of the dough around to the bottom on all four sides, rotating the ball a quarter-turn as you go.

3. Flatten the mass of dough to a thickness of about ½ inch on a wooden board dusted with flour and sprinkle it with olives. Roll up the dough, jelly-roll style, then shape it into a ball. Form a flat round approximately

½ inch thick. Because you will need to be able to cut slits into the dough that do not immediately close up and re-adhere to each other, this dough needs to be drier than most; so use flour accordingly. Place the round on a wooden board liberally dusted with flour.

4. Cut angled slits into the circle of dough (see photo below). You may need to add more flour to be able to cut the slits and keep them spread adequately during baking so they don't close up. Gently pull the holes to open them.

5. Gently lift the slitted dough round onto the prepared greased cookie sheet and brush additional olive oil onto the dough. Allow it to rest for 20 minutes.

6. Place the cookie sheet with the *fougasse* near the middle of the oven. Pour 1 cup of hot tap water into the broiler tray and quickly close the oven door. Check for doneness at about 20 minutes and continue baking, as needed, until golden brown, which may be 5 minutes longer. *Fougasse* will not develop a crackling crust because of the olive oil.

7. Serve warm.

Fougasse Stuffed with Roasted Red Pepper

This is a very festive folded flatbread with a roasted red pepper filling. It uses some of the same techniques used in making the olive *fougasse*, but the dough is folded after slitting, on one side only, to reveal the roasted red pepper layered inside (see color photo insert). The rich and smoky red pepper perfumes the whole loaf. It's a fantastic and impressive hors d'oeuvre, sliced or just broken into pieces.

Makes 6 appetizer portions

Use any of these refrigerated pre-mixed doughs: Olive Oil (page 134), Boule (page 26), European Peasant (page 46), Light Whole Wheat (page 74), or Italian Semolina (page 80)

1 pound (grapefruit-size portion) of any pre-mixed dough listed above

1 medium red bell pepper (or substitute equivalent amount of jarred roasted red pepper, drained and patted dry)

Coarse salt, for sprinkling

¼ teaspoon dried thyme

Olive oil, preferably extra virgin, for brushing the loaf

Whole wheat flour for covering the pizza peel

1. Cut the bell pepper into quarters and then flatten the pieces, making additional cuts if needed to flatten.

2. Grill or broil the pepper under the broiler or on a gas or charcoal grill, with the skin side closest to the heat source. Check often and remove when the skin is blackened, 8 to 10 minutes or more, depending on the heat source.

3. Drop the roasted pieces into an empty bowl and cover. The skin will loosen from the steam over the next 10 minutes.

4. Gently hand-peel the pepper and discard the blackened skin; some dark bits will adhere to the pepper's flesh, which is fine.

5. **Twenty minutes before baking time, preheat the oven to 450°F,** with a baking stone placed near the middle of the oven. Place an empty broiler tray on any other shelf that won't interfere with the rising bread.

6. Dust the surface of the refrigerated dough with flour and cut off a 1-pound (grapefruit-size) piece. Dust the piece with more flour and quickly shape it into a ball by stretching the surface of the dough around to the bottom on all four sides, rotating the ball a quarter-turn as you go.

7. Using a rolling pin, form a large flat round approximately ⅛ inch thick. Add a little more flour than usual when cloaking, shaping, and rolling the dough, because you will need to be able to cut slits into the dough that do not close and immediately re-adhere to one another. Place the round on a whole wheat–covered pizza peel.

8. Cut angled slits into the circle of dough *on only one half of the round* (see photo below). You may need to add more flour to decrease stickiness so the slits stay open during handling. Gently spread the holes open with your fingers.

9. Cut the roasted pepper into strips, and place in a single layer on the unslit side of the *fougasse,* leaving a 1-inch border at the edge. Sprinkle with coarse salt and thyme. Dampen the dough edge, fold the slitted side over to cover the peppers, and pinch to seal. The peppers should peek brightly through the slitted windows. Brush the loaf with olive oil.

10. Slide the *fougasse* directly onto the hot stone. Pour 1 cup of hot tap water into the broiler tray, and quickly close the oven door. Bake for about 25 minutes, or until golden brown.

11. Allow to cool, then slice or break into pieces and serve.

Sweet Provençal Flatbread with Anise Seeds

Provençal bakers are justly famous for their savory flatbreads such as *Pissaladière* (page 148), but their lesser-known, gently sweetened breads are just as delicious. The anise, which has a distinctive licorice flavor, is a perfect complement to the orange zest.

Makes about four 1-pound loaves or 8 small triangular loaves. The recipe is easily doubled or halved.

2¼ cups water
½ cup orange juice
¼ cup olive oil
1½ tablespoons granulated yeast (1½ packets)
1½ tablespoons salt
1 tablespoon whole anise seeds for dough, plus more for topping
⅓ cup sugar
Zest from half an orange
6½ cups all-purpose flour
Cornmeal for the pizza peel
Cornstarch wash (see sidebar, page 51)

1. **Mixing and storing the dough:** Mix together the yeast, salt, anise seeds, sugar, and orange zest with all the liquid ingredients in a 5-quart bowl, or a lidded (not airtight) food container.

2. Mix in the flour without kneading, using a spoon, a 14-cup capacity food processor (with dough attachment), or a heavy-duty stand mixer (with dough hook). If you're not using a machine, you may need to use wet hands to incorporate the last bit of flour.

3. Cover (not airtight), and allow to rest at room temperature until the dough rises and collapses (or flattens on top), approximately 2 hours.

4. The dough can be used immediately after the initial rise, though it is easier to handle when cold. Refrigerate in a lidded (not airtight) container and use over the next 14 days.

5. **On baking day,** dust the surface of the refrigerated dough with flour and cut off a 1-pound (grapefruit-size) piece. Dust the piece with more flour and quickly shape it into a ball by stretching the surface of the dough around to the bottom on all four sides, rotating the ball a quarter-turn as you go.

6. Flatten the ball with your hands and then, using a rolling pin and minimal dusting flour, roll out in a round with a uniform thickness of ½ inch. Cut the round into several triangles for an authentic Provençal look, or just form into a single round flatbread.

7. **Twenty minutes before baking time, preheat the oven to 450°F,** with a baking stone placed on the middle rack. Place an empty broiler tray on any other shelf that won't interfere with the rising bread.

8. Allow the bread to rest and rise on a cornmeal-covered pizza peel for 20 minutes. Just before baking, paint the surface with cornstarch wash and sprinkle with additional anise seeds. If you have shaped a single large loaf, slash it with a serrated knife.

9. Slide the loaf/loaves directly onto the hot stone. Pour 1 cup of hot tap water into the broiler tray, and quickly close the oven door. Bake for 15 to 20 minutes, or until richly browned and firm.

10. Allow to cool before eating.

Pine Nut–Studded Polenta Flatbread

Here's another recipe that plays with some classic Italian flavors: pine nuts, polenta, and olive oil. Polenta, coarse-ground Northern Italian–style cornmeal, creates a marvelous texture and crunch, the pine nuts add richness and flavor, and olive oil pulls it all together. You can make this with *Broa* dough (page 82), but the flavor will be more subtle and the texture less crunchy. The bread is a natural for dipping into hearty soups, or for dips and hors d'oeuvres.

Makes four 1-pound loaves. The recipe is easily doubled or halved.

3 cups water
1½ tablespoons granulated yeast (1½ packets)
1½ tablespoons salt
½ cup pine nuts
¾ cup ground polenta meal
5¾ cups all-purpose flour
Olive oil for brushing the top

1. **Mixing and storing the dough:** Mix the yeast, salt, and pine nuts with the water in a 5-quart bowl, or a lidded (not airtight) food container.

2. Mix in the remaining dry ingredients without kneading, using a spoon, a 14-cup capacity food processor (with dough attachment), or a heavy-duty stand mixer (with dough hook). If you're not using a machine, you may need to use wet hands to incorporate the last bit of flour.

3. Cover (not airtight), and allow to rest at room temperature until the dough rises and collapses (or flattens on top), approximately 2 hours.

4. The dough can be used immediately after the initial rise, though it is easier to handle when cold. Refrigerate in a lidded (not airtight) container and use over the next 8 days.

5. **On baking day**, dust the surface of the refrigerated dough with flour and cut off a 1-pound (grapefruit-size) piece. Dust the piece with more flour and quickly shape it into a ball by stretching the surface of the dough around to the bottom on all four sides, rotating the ball a quarter-turn as you go.

6. Flatten the ball and shape a 1-inch-thick, free-form loaf. Place on a cornmeal or polenta-covered pizza peel. Press the pine nuts back into the dough if they're peeking out (they will burn if directly exposed to oven heat). Brush with olive oil. Allow to rest and rise for 40 minutes.

7. **Twenty minutes before baking time, preheat the oven to 400°F**, with a baking stone placed on the middle rack. Place an empty broiler tray on any other shelf that won't interfere with the rising bread.

8. Slide the loaf directly onto the hot stone. Pour 1 cup of hot tap water into the broiler tray, and quickly close the oven door. Bake for about 20 minutes, or until richly browned and firm.

9. Allow to cool before eating.

Za'atar Flatbread

Za'atar spice has a lemony earthiness that is a bracing departure from everyday Western flavors. The distinctive taste comes from the ground sumac berries mixed with dried thyme and sesame seeds. You can blend your own or buy it at a Middle Eastern market (If you can't find it locally, try Penzey's Spices by mail order or online, where it is spelled "*zatar*"). To make your own, mix together 1 part ground sumac berries, 2 parts dried thyme, and 1 part sesame seeds.

"I first had za'atar bread in Minneapolis at an Iraqi grocery. The flavor of the spice mixture was so memorable that years later I returned to find the stuff and bake my own. The shopkeeper smiled at my pronunciation, but I was now the proud owner of a very reasonably priced three-year supply of za'atar."—Jeff

Don't worry if you end up with a large supply of *za'atar* spice blend—we have more recipes in the book where you can use it up. Jim's Spicy Kebabs (page 165) and *Fattoush*, the beautiful bread salad (page 166) are two Mediterranean dishes that get their exciting flavor from *za'atar*.

Makes 1 flatbread

Use any of these refrigerated pre-mixed doughs: Boule (page 26), European Peasant (page 46), Light Whole Wheat (page 74), Olive Oil (page 134), or Italian Semolina (page 80)
1 pound (grapefruit-size portion) of any pre-mixed dough listed above
3 tablespoons high-quality extra virgin olive oil, plus more for greasing the pan
1 tablespoon *za'atar* spice mix (see headnote above)
Coarse salt to taste

1. Grease a cookie sheet with a bit of olive oil and set aside. Dust the surface of the refrigerated dough with flour and cut off a 1-pound (grapefruit-size) piece. Dust the piece with more flour and quickly shape it into a ball by stretching the surface of the dough around to the bottom on all four sides, rotating the ball a quarter-turn as you go.

2. Flatten the ball into a round, approximately ½ to ¾ inch thick. Place the round on an olive oil-greased cookie sheet.

3. Sprinkle the *za'atar* spice mix over the dough round. Using your fingertips, poke holes into the surface of the dough at approximately one-inch intervals. The holes may partially "re-fill" with dough as soon as fingers are removed.

4. Drizzle the oil over the surface of the dough, taking care to fill indentations that remain from your finger-poking (do this even if you've started with olive oil dough). Some of the oil will run off the surface and find its way under the bread. Finish with a sprinkling of coarse salt, which strikingly accentuates the sourness of the *za'atar*. Use salt sparingly if your *za'atar* spice blend already contains salt.

5. **Twenty minutes before baking time, preheat the oven to 450°F.** Place an empty broiler tray on any other shelf that won't interfere with the flatbread. The baking stone is not essential with the cookie sheet; if you omit it the preheat may be as short as 5 minutes.

6. After the *za'atar* bread has rested 20 minutes, place the cookie sheet on a rack near the center of the oven. Pour 1 cup of hot tap water into the broiler tray and quickly close the oven door.

7. Check for doneness at 15 minutes, and continue baking until medium brown. The baking time will vary according to the thickness of the *za'atar* bread. *Za'atar* bread does not develop a crackling crust because of its oil content, but the final color should be a medium brown.

8. Cut into wedges and serve warm.

Pita

Pita bread is the puffy, flour-dusted flatbread of the Middle East. It is a simple and elemental bread, and for reasons we can't explain at all, it's just about our most fragrant one. Aside from being delicious, this bread is among the fastest in the book to make. It's quite easy to produce beautiful puffed loaves. The secret to the puffing is to roll the dough thinly and use a very hot oven. Because pita isn't slashed, internal steam is trapped inside. As soon as the top and bottom crusts set, steam in the interior pushes them apart. It can't miss! And this is a bread that when still warm from the oven is best.

"My friend Jim has become something of an expert on great pita, because his job takes him to the Middle East all the time. When he invited my family to his cabin in northern Minnesota, he asked me to prepare pita to accompany a kebab dish he was making—a special recipe he'd fallen for overseas. It was a delicious incongruity: hot and spicy food from the desert, served with pita, in northern Minnesota in January. We cross-country skied and hiked all day on the lake, not around it. As the northern sun started to wane, Jim drove out on the ice to summon me back to the kitchen to start on the breads. We made the za'atar flatbread as an appetizer, and puffed pita for Jim's kebabs. The flavors and smells of the Mediterranean transported us to a different, warmer place."—Jeff

Makes 1 large family-style pita, or 4 individual pitas

Use any of these refrigerated pre-mixed doughs: Boule (page 26), European Peasant (page 46), Light Whole Wheat (page 74), or Italian Semolina (page 80)
1 pound (grapefruit-size portion) of any pre-mixed dough listed above
Flour for dusting

1. **Twenty minutes before baking, preheat the oven to 500°F with a baking stone.** You won't be using a broiler tray and shelf placement of the stone is not crucial.

2. Just before baking, dust the surface of the refrigerated dough with

flour and cut off a 1-pound (grapefruit-size) piece. Dust the piece with more flour and quickly shape it into a ball by stretching the surface of the dough around to the bottom on all four sides, rotating the ball a quarter-turn as you go. Place the dough on a flour-dusted pizza peel.

3. Using your hands and a rolling pin, roll the dough out into a round with a uniform thickness of ⅛ inch throughout. This is crucial, because if it's too thick, it may not puff. You'll need to sprinkle the peel lightly with white flour as you work, occasionally flipping the bread to prevent sticking to the rolling pin or to the board. Use a dough scraper to remove the round of dough from the peel if it sticks. Do not slash the pita or it will not puff. No rest/rise time is needed. (If you are making individual pitas, form, roll, and shape the rest.)

4. If you have a ventilation fan, turn it on now because stray flour may smoke at this temperature. Slide the loaf directly onto the hot stone (it may take a number of back-and-forth shakes to dislodge the pita). Bake for about 5 to 7 minutes, until lightly browned and puffed. You may need to transfer the pita to a higher shelf (without the stone) to achieve browning.

5. For the most authentic, soft-crusted result, wrap in clean cotton dish towels and set on a cooling rack when baking is complete. The pitas will deflate slightly as they cool. The space between crusts will still be there, but may have to be nudged apart with a fork.

6. Serve the pita with Jim's Spicy Kebabs (recipe follows). Or, once the pitas are cool, store in plastic bags. Unlike hard-crusted breads, pita is not harmed by airtight storage.

Jim's Spicy Kebabs

Jim re-created the flavors he fondly remembered from the Middle East. The meat combination yields succulent morsels, and they're a perfect fit for oven-fresh pita.

Serves 4 to 6

1½ pounds ground meat (half lamb and half veal, or all lamb)
2 teaspoons cayenne pepper
2 teaspoons ground cumin seeds
2 teaspoons ground coriander seeds
2 teaspoons ground pepper
Salt to taste
Ground sumac or mixed *za'atar* spice (see page 161), to taste, optional
1 medium Vidalia, Spanish, red, or other sweet onion, thinly sliced
Finely chopped fresh parsley
4 to 6 individual pitas

1. Mix all the ingredients except the sumac, onions, parsley, and pitas. Cover and let the mixture rest in the refrigerator for 1 hour.

2. Prepare a charcoal fire or preheat a gas grill on medium-low for 15 minutes. Form the meat into elongated patties and grill, without overcooking and turning often, until the kebabs are springy to the touch, about 20 minutes.

3. Fill the pita halves with the patties and sprinkle lightly with sumac. Top with the sliced onions and garnish with chopped parsley.

Fattoush

This Lebanese bread salad is as beautiful to look at as it is to eat, with all its rich colors and exotic Middle Eastern flavors. *Fattoush* is related to other Mediterranean bread salads like Tuscan *Panzanella* (page 48), which is always based on European bread. This Lebanese specialty has some differences from the Tuscan variety. The flavor is defined by lemon juice, mint, parsley, and, if you have it, sumac or *za'atar* (see Za'atar Flatbread, page 161). The salad calls for Middle Eastern pita bread (page 163), which is used fresh and toasted, rather than stale as in *Panzanella*—stale pitas turn into hockey pucks when you toast them!

Makes 4 servings

The Salad

3 medium tomatoes, cubed

1 medium cucumber, chopped

1 scallion, sliced into rings

2 large romaine lettuce leaves, torn into bite-size pieces

⅓ cup finely chopped parsley

3 tablespoons chopped fresh mint, or 1 tablespoon dried

2 pita (page 163), about 6 to 8 inches across, toasted crisp and cut into bite-size chunks

The Dressing

⅓ cup extra virgin olive oil

Juice of ½ lemon

1 garlic clove, finely minced

1 teaspoon salt

Freshly ground pepper to taste

1 teaspoon ground sumac or *za'atar* (see page 161)

1. Prepare all the ingredients for the salad and place in a large salad bowl.

2. Whisk all the ingredients for the dressing until well combined.

3. Pour the dressing over the salad and allow to stand for at least 10 minutes, or until the bread has softened.

Lavash

Armenian *lavash* is believed to be among the world's oldest breads, dating back as many as ten thousand years. This simple flatbread makes a great vehicle to mop up sauces, or serve with soups and dips.

The small amount of dough goes a long way because it's rolled so thin. There are thicker versions from other parts of Central Asia as well as superthin cracker versions. We pull our *lavash* from the oven when only lightly browned and still chewy. Like so many other things, this is a matter of taste, so if you're looking for a cracker bread, bake it until deep brown and crispy. Experiment with several doughs. This is a very versatile recipe.

The flavors that hit you in our *lavash* are sesame seeds and the bread's light caramelization. The combination outweighs the usual "wheatiness" of most breads, making this a very unique, yet subtle flavor experience.

Makes several lavash

Use any of these refrigerated pre-mixed doughs: Boule (page 26), European
  Peasant (page 46), Light Whole Wheat (page 74), Italian Semolina (page
  80), or Olive Oil (page 134)
½ pound (orange-size portion) of any pre-mixed dough listed above
Sesame seeds for top crust
Cornstarch wash (see sidebar, page 51)

1. **Twenty minutes before baking, preheat the oven to 450°F,** with a
    baking stone. Place an empty broiler tray on any other shelf that won't
    interfere with the bread.

2. Meanwhile, dust the surface of the refrigerated dough with flour and
    cut off a half-pound (orange-size) piece. Dust the piece with more
    flour and quickly shape it into a ball by stretching the surface of the
    dough around to the bottom on all four sides, rotating the ball a
    quarter-turn as you go.

3. Place the dough on a pizza peel and shape it into a flat round, using your hands and a rolling pin. Continue rolling out the bread on the peel until you reach a uniform thickness of $\frac{1}{16}$ to $\frac{1}{8}$ inch throughout. You'll be able to make several *lavash* from your half-pound piece of dough.

4. Brush the top surface with cornstarch wash and sprinkle with sesame seeds. Prick the surface all over with a fork to allow steam to escape and prevent puffing. There's no need for resting time.

5. Slide the *lavash* directly onto the hot stone. Pour 1 cup of hot tap water into the broiler tray, and quickly close the oven door. Bake for about 5 minutes, or until lightly browned. Do not overbrown; you're not trying to crisp the bread.

6. *Lavash* cools quickly; but can be served warm. Once cool, it stores very well in plastic bags. Unlike hard-crusted breads, *lavash* is not harmed by airtight storage.

Ksra (Moroccan Anise and Barley Flatbread)

This is a very hearty and satisfying country bread that is virtually unknown in the United States. If you can't get rolled barley or barley flour, substitute whole wheat or rye flour; either will blend nicely with the anise. Moroccan flatbreads are thicker than *lavash* and pita. We make ours about the same thickness as our focaccia.

"I first tasted Ksra on a bus in 1987. The bus, however, was 1960s vintage, and it bumped painfully over the Atlas Mountains of Morocco. The rest stops didn't include restaurants, the bus was freezing at high altitude, and the ride was much longer than billed, so I was starving. At a rest stop, I bought some ksra from a street vendor. If you're going to live through an adventure like this on bread and water for 16 hours, this is the most delicious way to do it. The heartiness of the barley made it feel like a meal."—Jeff

Makes four 1-pound loaves. The recipe is easily doubled or halved.

3 cups lukewarm water
1½ tablespoons granulated yeast (1½ packets)
1½ tablespoons salt
1 tablespoon whole anise seeds
¾ cup rolled barley or barley flour (whole wheat or rye can be substituted)
5¾ cups unbleached all-purpose flour

1. **Mixing and storing the dough:** Mix the yeast, salt, and anise seeds with the water in a 3-quart bowl, or a lidded (not airtight) food container.

2. Mix in flours without kneading, using a spoon, a 14-cup capacity food processor (with dough attachment), or a heavy-duty stand mixer (with dough hook). If you're not using a machine, you may need to use wet hands to incorporate the last bit of flour.

3. Cover (not airtight), and allow to rest at room temperature until the dough rises and collapses (or flattens on top), approximately 2 hours.

4. The dough can be used immediately after the initial rise, though it is easier to handle when cold. Refrigerate in a lidded (not airtight) container and use over the next 10 days.

5. **On baking day, preheat the oven to 450°F,** with a baking stone placed on the middle rack. Place an empty broiler tray on any other shelf that won't interfere with the bread.

6. Dust the surface of the refrigerated dough with flour and cut off a 1-pound (grapefruit-size) piece. Dust the piece with more flour and quickly shape it into a ball by stretching the surface of the dough around to the bottom on all four sides, rotating the ball a quarter-turn as you go.

7. Flatten the dough into a ¾-inch-thick round and allow to rest and rise on a cornmeal-covered pizza peel for 20 minutes.

8. Slide the loaf directly onto the hot stone. Pour 1 cup of hot tap water into the broiler tray, and quickly close the oven door. Bake for about 20 minutes, or until richly browned and firm.

9. Allow to cool, cut into wedges, and serve.

Chilled Moroccan-Style Gazpacho

Of course, one cannot really live on *ksra* and water alone, so here's something to go with our hearty Moroccan bread (see previous recipe). We love the light, refreshing coolness of garden-fresh *gazpacho* on a summer evening, but we wanted a soup that was more like a meal. We borrowed the chickpeas and spicy *harissa* paste from Moroccan *harira* soup and *voilà*! A smooth, tangy chilled soup with a North African accent.

Makes 4 servings

3 ripe medium tomatoes
½ medium cucumber, roughly chopped
1 red bell pepper, roughly chopped
2 slices bread
½ small onion, roughly chopped
2 cloves garlic, roughly chopped
2 tablespoons red wine vinegar
⅓ cup extra virgin olive oil
½ teaspoon ground cumin
1 teaspoon salt
Freshly ground black pepper to taste
3 teaspoons *harissa* paste (available from Middle Eastern groceries)
¼ cup chopped cilantro
1 can chickpeas, well-drained

1. Place all ingredients except chickpeas into the bowl of a food processor and process until desired consistency; we like ours a bit chunky, but purists will insist it should be smooth—your choice.

2. Add chickpeas and allow to stand for one-half hour in the refrigerator. Adjust seasonings just before eating.

Naan

This delicious and buttery Indian flatbread is traditionally made in a huge cylindrical clay tandoori oven, with the wet dough slapped directly onto the oven's hot walls. Our naan is done in a hot, cast-iron skillet, or a heavyweight nonstick skillet. Butter or oil will work in lieu of authentic Indian clarified butter *(ghee)*, but the taste won't be as authentic. You can find ghee at South Asian or Middle Eastern markets.

This recipe also has the distinction of producing the fastest bread in the book, since it's done on the stovetop without an oven preheat (*lavash* and pita are close seconds). As with many of our flatbreads, there's no need to rest the dough. You can easily make one of these just before dinner, even on busy nights (so long as you have the dough in the fridge). Try it with Suvir Saran's Chilled Yogurt Soup with Cucumber and Mint (page 175).

"Naan has become my family's favorite bread to make while camping in the woods. All we need is a 12-inch cast-iron skillet on our sturdy Coleman stove to have freshly baked bread. We always attract a crowd of curious campers drawn to the aroma wafting amidst the wood smoke."—Jeff

Makes 1 naan

Use any of these refrigerated pre-mixed doughs: Boule (page 26), European Peasant (page 46), Light Whole Wheat (page 74), Italian Semolina (page 80)
¼ pound (peach-size portion) of any pre-mixed dough listed above
1 tablespoon *ghee* (commercial or homemade), or neutral-flavored oil
Butter for brushing on loaf if *ghee* is unavailable

1. Dust the surface of the refrigerated dough with flour and cut off a ¼-pound (peach-size) piece. Dust the piece with more flour and quickly shape it into a ball by stretching the surface of the dough around to the bottom on all four sides, rotating the ball a quarter-turn as you go. Using your hands and a rolling pin, and minimal flour, roll out to a uniform thickness of ⅛ inch throughout and to a diameter of 8 to 9 inches.

2. Heat a heavy 12-inch cast-iron skillet over high heat on the stovetop. When water droplets flicked into the pan skitter across the surface and evaporate quickly the pan is ready. Add the *ghee* or oil, pouring out excess fat if necessary.

3. Drop the rolled dough round into the skillet, decrease the heat to medium, and cover the skillet to trap the steam and heat.

4. Check for doneness with a spatula at about 3 minutes, or sooner if you're smelling overly quick browning. Adjust the heat as needed. Flip the naan when the underside is richly browned.

5. Continue cooking another 2 to 6 minutes, or until the naan feels firm, even at the edges, and the second side is browned. If you've rolled a thicker naan, or if you're using dough with whole grains, you'll need more pan time.

6. Remove the naan from the pan, brush with butter if the dough was cooked in oil, and serve.

Suvir Saran's Chilled Yogurt Soup with Cucumber and Mint

"My friend Suvir Saran, chef/owner of the acclaimed New York restaurant Dévi, ingeniously merges very traditional Indian flavors with the most sophisticated modern cuisine. This recipe comes from his sublime book Indian Home Cooking. *The cool and soothing yogurt blended with bracing spices is a provocative way to start off a summertime meal, served with fresh, soft* naan, *glistening with* ghee *(see previous recipe)."—Zoë*

Makes 4 servings

1½ teaspoons cumin seeds
3½ cups plain yogurt
1 medium cucumber, roughly chopped
1 small fresh hot green chili, such as serrano, seeded and finely chopped
¼ teaspoon *garam masala*
1 teaspoon salt, or to taste
⅛ teaspoon freshly ground white pepper
3 tablespoons roughly chopped fresh mint leaves, plus 12 additional whole
  leaves for garnish

1. Toast the cumin seeds in a dry frying pan or saucepan over medium heat for 2 to 3 minutes, until lightly browned and fragrant. Grind to a powder in a spice grinder.

2. Reserving a small amount of cumin powder for the garnish, combine all ingredients except the whole mint leaves in a food processor and process until smooth. Scrape the mixture into a serving bowl. Refrigerate at least one-half hour, until chilled.

3. To serve, garnish with whole mint leaves and sprinkle with ground cumin, if desired.

Flatbrød

We developed a quick version of traditional Scandinavian rye crisp bread. It is usually baked unadorned, but in an unorthodox mood we added some Mediterranean zest by topping it with olive oil and coarse salt. Unlike our *lavash*, *flatbrød* is rolled out paper-thin, then baked till crisp and browned. Top with smoked fish, herring, capers, or other Scandinavian delicacies and serve.

Makes several sheets of crisp flatbrød

½ pound (orange-size portion) Deli-Style Rye dough (page 58), mixed
    without caraway seeds
Olive oil for brushing
Coarse salt for sprinkling

1. **Twenty minutes before baking, preheat the oven to 375°F,** with a baking stone. Place an empty broiler tray on any other shelf that won't interfere with the cracker.

2. Dust the surface of the refrigerated dough with flour and cut off a half-pound (orange-size) piece. Dust the piece with more flour and quickly shape it into a ball by stretching the surface of the dough around to the bottom on all four sides, rotating the ball a quarter-turn as you go.

3. Place the dough on a pizza peel and shape the dough into a flat round, approximately 1 inch thick. Cut the dough into several small pieces and roll out on the pizza peel until it is paper-thin, adding all-purpose flour as needed. You should be able to make several *flatbrød* from your half-pound piece of dough.

4. Brush the breads with olive oil and sprinkle with coarse salt. Prick the surface all over with a fork to allow steam to escape and prevent puffing. There's no need for resting time.

5. Slide the *flatbrød* directly onto the hot stone. Pour 1 cup of hot tap water into the broiler tray, and quickly close the oven door. Check for puffing at 1 minute; if you see any large bubbles puffing up, prick them with a sharp fork. Bake the breads for 2 to 5 minutes, or until richly browned and crisp. Repeat the process to make the rest of the crisp breads.

6. Allow to cool on a rack and break into serving-size portions.

8

ENRICHED BREADS AND PASTRIES

∽

We're particularly pleased to present great sweet enriched breads and pastries made from stored dough. If you keep enriched dough in your freezer, you'll be able to store it for weeks. Then, create great morning pastries, coffee cakes, holiday breads, and late-night chocolate fixes on the spur of the moment. Though some of them need a few minutes more preparation than our regular breads, they're all based on dough that will be stored, so the preparation time will be a fraction of what you're used to with traditional pastries, and you'll have wonderful results. Enjoy!

Challah

This is the bread traditionally served in Jewish households at the start of the Sabbath on Friday nights. Some variation of an egg-enriched sweet loaf appears across bread-loving cultures. The French and Italians have Brioche (page 189). The choice of melted butter versus oil definitely changes the flavor and aroma. And butter-enriched doughs are stiffer and easier to braid when cold; oil-based challah dough is a little "looser" and more prone to spreading sideways while resting, but delicious nonetheless. For an intense and decadent challah, try making it with Brioche dough. The blast of butter and egg creates an incredibly rich bread-eating experience.

We store the egg-enriched dough in the freezer after 5 days of refrigerator storage.

Makes four 1-pound loaves. The recipe is easily doubled or halved.

1¾ cups lukewarm water
1½ tablespoons granulated yeast (1½ packets)
1½ tablespoons salt
4 large eggs, lightly beaten
½ cup honey
½ cup unsalted butter, melted (or neutral-tasting vegetable oil such as canola), plus more for greasing the cookie sheet
7 cups unbleached all-purpose flour
Egg wash (1 egg beaten with 1 tablespoon of water)
Poppy or sesame seeds for the top

1. **Mixing and storing the dough:** Mix the yeast, salt, eggs, honey, and melted butter (or oil) with the water in a 5-quart bowl, or a lidded (not airtight) food container.

2. Mix in the flour without kneading, using a spoon, a 14-cup capacity food processor (with dough attachment), or a heavy-duty stand mixer

(with dough hook). If you're not using a machine, you may need to use wet hands to incorporate the last bit of flour.

3. Cover (not airtight), and allow to rest at room temperature until the dough rises and collapses (or flattens on top), approximately 2 hours.

4. The dough can be used immediately after the initial rise, though it is easier to handle when cold. Refrigerate in a lidded (not airtight) container and use over the next 5 days. Beyond 5 days, freeze in 1-pound portions in an airtight container for up to 4 weeks. Defrost frozen dough overnight in the refrigerator before using. Then allow the usual rest and rise time.

5. **On baking day,** butter or grease a cookie sheet or line with parchment paper or a silicone mat. Dust the surface of the refrigerated dough with flour and cut off a 1-pound (grapefruit-size) piece. Dust the piece with more flour and quickly shape it into a ball by stretching the surface of the dough around to the bottom on all four sides, rotating the ball a quarter-turn as you go.

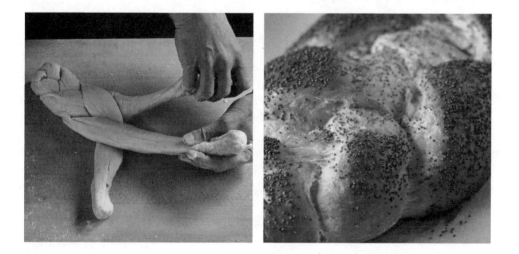

6. Divide the ball into thirds, using a dough scraper or knife. Roll the balls between your hands (or on a board), stretching, to form each into a long, thin rope. If the dough resists shaping, let it rest for 5 minutes and try again. Braid the ropes, starting from the center and working to one end. Turn the loaf over, rotate it, and braid from the center out to the remaining end. This produces a loaf with a more uniform thickness than when braided from end to end.

7. Allow the bread to rest and rise on the prepared cookie sheet for 1 hour and 20 minutes (or just 40 minutes if you're using fresh, unrefrigerated dough).

8. **Twenty minutes before baking time, preheat the oven to 350°F.** If you're not using a stone in the oven, 5 minutes is adequate. Brush the loaf with egg wash and sprinkle with the seeds.

9. Bake near the center of the oven for about 25 minutes. Smaller or larger loaves will require adjustments in baking time. The challah is done when golden brown, and the braids near the center of the loaf offer resistance to pressure. Due to the fat in the dough, challah will not form a hard, crackling crust.

10. Allow to cool before slicing or eating.

Turban-Shaped Challah with Raisins

Turban-Shaped Raisin Challah is served at the Jewish New Year, but similar enriched and fruited egg breads are part of holiday traditions all over the Western world, calling to mind the richer Italian Pannetone, served at Christmas (page 201).

We've assumed in this recipe that you're using stored challah dough and rolling the raisins into it. If you're starting a batch of dough just for raisin challah, add three-quarters of a cup of raisins to the yeasted water when mixing.

Makes 1 challah

Use any of these refrigerated pre-mixed doughs: Challah (page 180) or
  Brioche (page 189)
1 pound (grapefruit-size portion) of any pre-mixed dough listed above,
  defrosted overnight in refrigerator if frozen
Butter for greasing cookie sheet
¼ cup raisins
Egg wash (1 egg beaten with 1 tablespoon of water)
Sesame seeds for the top

1. Defrost the dough overnight in the refrigerator if frozen. **On baking day,** grease a cookie sheet or line with parchment paper or a silicone mat. Dust the surface of the refrigerated dough with flour and cut off a 1-pound (grapefruit-size) piece. Dust the piece with more flour and quickly shape it into a ball by stretching the surface of the dough around to the bottom on all four sides, rotating the ball a quarter-turn as you go.

2. Using a rolling pin and minimal dusting flour, roll out the dough to a thickness of ½ inch. Sprinkle with the raisins and roll into a log.

3. Rolling the dough between your hands and stretching it, form a single long, thin rope, tapering it at one end. If the dough resists shaping, let it rest for 5 minutes and try again.

4. Starting with the thick end of the rope, begin forming a coil on the prepared cookie sheet. When you have finished coiling, pinch the thin end under the loaf. Allow to rest and rise for 1 hour and 20 minutes (or just 40 minutes if you're using fresh, unrefrigerated dough).

5. **Twenty minutes before baking time, preheat the oven to 350°F.** If you're not using a stone in the oven, 5 minutes is adequate.

6. Brush the loaf with egg wash and sprinkle with seeds, and place near the center of the oven. Bake for about 25 minutes. The challah is done when golden brown and the center of the loaf offers resistance to pressure. Smaller or larger loaves will require adjustments in baking time. Due to the fat in the dough, challah will not form a hard, crackling crust.

7. Allow to cool before slicing or eating.

John Barrymore Onion Pletzel

"*Pletzel*" or "*pletzl*" is a Yiddish word meaning "board." It was a savory flat-bread widely available in Jewish bakeries until about twenty-five years ago. The *pletzel* flavors are a unique blend of onions and poppy seeds baked onto enriched and slightly sweetened dough. It is an Eastern European savory treat that is unforgettable when served with pot-roasted meats. *Pletzel* is perfect for mopping up that home-style gravy.

"For reasons that are to this day unclear, my grandfather called this bread "John Barrymore Pletzel." It's too bad I didn't question him about it during his lifetime. I find absolutely no connection between the actor John Barrymore and any bread, let alone pletzel.

"This is one of my most vivid taste memories from childhood. Twenty years elapsed between the last time I ate it and the first time I baked it, but the flavor is exactly what I recalled."—Jeff

Makes 2 pletzel

Use any of these refrigerated pre-mixed doughs: Challah (page 180) or
    Brioche (page 189)
1 pound (grapefruit-size portion) of any pre-mixed dough listed above,
    defrosted overnight in refrigerator if frozen
1½ tablespoons neutral-tasting oil or butter, plus more for greasing the pan
1 small onion, thinly sliced
2 teaspoons poppy seeds
¼ teaspoon salt

1. **On baking day,** grease a cookie sheet or line with parchment paper or
    a silicone mat. Set aside. Dust the surface of the refrigerated dough
    with flour and cut off a 1-pound (grapefruit-size) piece. Dust the
    piece with more flour and quickly shape it into a ball by stretching the
    surface of the dough around to the bottom on all four sides, rotating
    the ball a quarter-turn as you go.

2. Using a rolling pin or your hands, flatten the dough to a thickness of ½ inch and place on the prepared cookie sheet. (Alternatively, press the unrolled dough into a well-greased, square 9×9-inch nonstick baking pan.) Allow to rest and rise 20 minutes.

3. **Twenty minutes before baking time, preheat the oven to 350°F.** If you're not using a stone in the oven, 5 minutes is adequate.

4. Meanwhile, sauté the onion in the oil or butter until very lightly browned; don't overbrown, or they will burn in the oven. Strew the onions onto the *pletzel* and drizzle oil or butter over them (don't completely cover the surface with onions or the *pletzel* won't brown well). Finish by sprinkling the poppy seeds and salt over the onions.

5. After the *pletzel* has rested, place the cookie sheet near the center of the oven. Bake for 15 to 20 minutes, or until the *pletzel* has browned but the onions are not burned.

6. Allow to cool, then cut into pieces before serving.

Sticky Pecan Caramel Rolls

This crowd-pleaser was our first attempt to make dessert from stored bread dough (see color photo insert). Stored bread dough? For dessert? We were skeptical, but our first attempt with sweet enriched dough, caramel, toasted nuts, and spices was so successful that it reshaped our view of what this cookbook would be. The flavors were actually enhanced by using stored dough. We've even used the Boule dough in this recipe, and it works! The butter and sugar in the filling and on the bottom of the pan seep into the folds and do a pretty good approximation of the egg-enriched version.

Makes 6 to 8 large caramel rolls

Use any of these refrigerated pre-mixed doughs: Challah (page 180), Brioche (page 189), or Boule (page 26)

1½ pounds (cantaloupe-size portion) of any pre-mixed dough listed above, defrosted overnight in the refrigerator if frozen

The Caramel Topping
6 tablespoons unsalted butter, softened
½ teaspoon salt
½ cup brown sugar
30 pecan halves

The Filling
4 tablespoons salted butter, softened
¼ cup sugar
1 teaspoon ground cinnamon
¼ teaspoon freshly grated nutmeg
½ cup chopped and toasted pecans
Pinch of ground black pepper

1. **On baking day,** cream together the butter, salt, and brown sugar. Spread evenly over the bottom of a 9-inch cake pan. Scatter the pecans over the butter-sugar mixture and set aside.

2. Dust the surface of the refrigerated dough with flour and cut off a
    1½-pound (cantaloupe-size) piece. Dust the piece with more flour
    and quickly shape it into a ball by stretching the surface of the dough
    around to the bottom on all four sides, rotating the ball a quarter-turn
    as you go.

3. With a rolling pin, roll out the dough to a ⅛-inch thick rectangle. As
    you roll out the dough, use enough flour to prevent it from sticking to
    the work surface but not so much as to make the dough dry.

4. Cream together the butter, sugar, and spices. Spread evenly over the
    rolled-out dough and sprinkle with the chopped nuts. Starting with
    the long side, roll the dough into a log. If the dough is too soft to cut,
    let it chill for 20 minutes to firm up.

5. With a very sharp serrated knife, cut the log into 8 equal pieces and
    arrange over the pecans in the pan, with the "swirled" edge facing
    upward. Cover loosely with plastic wrap and allow to rest and rise 1
    hour (or just 40 minutes if you're using fresh, unrefrigerated dough).

6. **Twenty minutes before baking time,
    preheat the oven to 350°F.** If you're not
    using a stone in the oven, 5 minutes is
    adequate.

7. Bake about 40 minutes, or until golden
    brown and well set in center. While still
    hot, run a knife around the inside of the
    pan to release the caramel rolls, and
    invert immediately onto a serving dish. If
    you let them set too long they will stick
    to the pan and be difficult to turn out.

Brioche

The doomed Marie Antoinette is often quoted as saying *"qu'ils mangent de la brioche,"* which means "let them eat brioche," not "let them eat cake (*gâteau*)"! Historians believe it was the insensitive remark of an earlier queen, but in any case it was brioche on their minds and not cake.

Brioche is a wonderful bread that everyone should eat. It is enjoyed as a sweet bread with tea or as a breakfast pastry. Brioche is rich with butter (use only fresh sweet cream butter, never oil), egg, and a touch of honey. It is perfect baked in a simple loaf pan or as a *Brioche à Tête* (page 191) and it is the inspiration for many of our pastry recipes (pages 191, 193, 195, 197, 199, 215, 219, 225, 228, 231, 233).

Makes four 1-pound loaves. The recipe is easily doubled or halved.

1½ cups lukewarm water
1½ tablespoons granulated yeast (1½ packets)
1½ tablespoons salt
8 eggs, lightly beaten
½ cup honey
1½ cups (3 sticks) unsalted butter, melted, plus butter for greasing the pan
7½ cups unbleached all-purpose flour
Egg wash (1 egg beaten with 1 tablespoon of water)

1. Mix the yeast, salt, eggs, honey, and melted butter with the water in a 5-quart bowl, or a lidded (not airtight) food container.

2. Mix in the flour without kneading, using a spoon, a 14-cup capacity food processor (with dough attachment), or a heavy-duty stand mixer (with dough hook). If you're not using a machine, you may need to use wet hands to incorporate the last bit of flour. The dough will be loose but will firm up when chilled; don't try to work with it before chilling. (You may notice lumps in the dough but they will disappear in the finished products.)

3. Cover (not airtight), and allow to rest at room temperature until dough rises and collapses (or flattens on top), approximately 2 hours.

4. The dough can be used as soon as it's chilled after the initial rise. Refrigerate in a lidded (not airtight) container and use over the next 5 days. Beyond 5 days, freeze the dough in 1-pound portions in an airtight container for up to 4 weeks. When using frozen dough, thaw in the refrigerator for 24 hours before using, then allow the usual rest and rise times.

5. Defrost the dough overnight in the refrigerator if frozen. **On baking day,** grease a 9×4×3-inch nonstick loaf pan. Dust the surface of the refrigerated dough with flour and cut off a 1-pound (grapefruit-size) piece. Dust the piece with more flour and quickly shape it into a ball by stretching the surface of the dough around to the bottom on all four sides, rotating the ball a quarter-turn as you go.

6. Elongate into an oval and place in the prepared pan. Allow to rest for 1 hour and 20 minutes.

7. **Twenty minutes before baking time, preheat the oven to 350°F.** If you're not using a stone in the oven, 5 minutes is adequate.

8. Using a pastry brush, brush the top crust with egg wash.

9. Place the bread near the center of the oven and bake for 35 to 40 minutes, or until a medium golden brown. Due to the fat in the dough, brioche will not form a hard, crackling crust.

10. Allow to cool before slicing or eating.

Brioche à Tête

Brioche à tête is a very traditional French bread loaf, baked in a beautifully fluted pan and sporting an extra little ball of dough at the top (the *tête*, or head—see color photo insert). Your guests will think you slaved over this one. The shape is ubiquitous in Parisian shops but quite rare elsewhere.

Makes 1 loaf

1 pound (grapefruit-size portion) Brioche dough (page 187), defrosted
   overnight in the refrigerator if frozen
Butter or oil for greasing the pan
Egg wash (1 egg beaten with 1 tablespoon of water)

1. Grease a brioche pan with a small amount of oil or butter.

2. Dust the surface of the refrigerated dough with flour and cut off a 1-pound (grapefruit-size) piece. Break off about an eighth of the dough to form the *tête* (head) and set it aside. Dust the large piece with more flour and quickly shape it into a ball by stretching the surface of the dough around to the bottom on all four sides, rotating the ball a quarter-turn as you go.

3. Place the larger ball into the prepared pan, seam side down; the pan should be about half-full. Poke a fairly deep indentation in the top of this ball of dough. This is where you will attach the *tête*.

4. Quickly shape the small piece into a teardrop shape by rounding one end and tapering the other. Place the teardrop, pointed side down, into the indentation of the dough in the pan and pinch the two together gently but firmly to ensure the *tête* stays attached during baking.

5. Allow to rest at room temperature for 1 hour and 20 minutes.

6. **Twenty minutes before baking time, preheat the oven to 350°F.** If you're not using a stone in the oven, 5 minutes is adequate.

7. Brush the loaf with egg wash and place it in the center of the oven. Bake for about 40 minutes, or until golden brown. The amount of dough and baking time will vary depending on the pan size.

Almond Brioche "Bostock"

We adore brioche "Bostock" with its combination of buttery brioche, almond cream, and orange zest–infused sugar. The traditional method involves baking brioche, slicing it, topping the slices with almond cream and re-baking it. But that's just too much work for our five-minutes-a-day cookbook. We wanted the flavors without the extra work, so we rolled the filling into the dough and baked it just once. It was fantastic!

Makes 1 loaf

1½ pounds (cantaloupe-size portion) Brioche dough (page 189), defrosted overnight in the refrigerator if frozen

4 tablespoons unsalted butter at room temperature, plus more for greasing the pan

½ cup almond paste

¼ cup unbleached all-purpose flour

1 egg

¼ teaspoon orange-flower water (optional)

¼ teaspoon almond extract

¼ cup sugar, plus more for dusting the greased pan

Zest from half an orange

½ cup sliced natural almonds (raw and unsalted)

1. **Making the almond cream:** Cream together the butter, almond paste, flour, egg, orange-flower water and almond extract in a food processor until smooth and well combined. Set aside.

2. **Assembling the brioche:** Dust the surface of the refrigerated dough with flour and cut off a 1½-pound (cantaloupe-size) piece. Dust the piece with more flour and quickly shape it into a ball by stretching the surface of the dough around to the bottom on all four sides, rotating the ball a quarter-turn as you go.

3. With a rolling pin, roll out the ball into a ¼-inch-thick rectangle. As you roll out the dough, use enough flour to prevent it from sticking to the work surface but not so much as to make the dough dry.

4. Spread the almond cream evenly over the rectangle, leaving a 1-inch border all around. Roll up the dough, jelly-roll style, starting at the long end, and being sure to seal the bare edges. The dough will be very soft, so chill the log for about 15 minutes in the freezer before cutting it in Step 6.

5. Generously grease an 8-inch round cake pan with butter. Sprinkle the greased pan with a dusting of granulated sugar.

6. Cut the chilled dough into 8 equal pieces. Place them evenly in the prepared cake pan so that the swirled cut edge is facing upward. Allow the dough to rest for 1 hour.

7. **Twenty minutes before baking time, preheat the oven to 350°F.** If you're not using a stone in the oven, 5 minutes is adequate.

8. Just before baking, mix together sugar, orange zest, and almonds and sprinkle over the brioche. Bake without steam until golden brown and well set in the center, about 40 minutes.

9. Run a knife around the inside of the pan to release the brioche while it is still hot and invert it onto a serving dish. If you let it set too long it will stick to the pan and be difficult to turn out. Eat warm.

Brioche Filled with Chocolate Ganache

This is the closest you'll ever get to the aroma of a Paris *pâtisserie* in your own kitchen. Using the best chocolate available makes a difference. As the bread bakes, the chocolate ganache will reveal itself and create a wonderfully rustic-looking loaf.

Makes 1 loaf

1 pound (grapefruit-size portion) Brioche dough (page 189), defrosted
   overnight in the refrigerator if frozen
¼ pound bittersweet chocolate (Valrhona or equivalent; page 12), finely
   chopped
2 tablespoons unsalted butter, plus more for greasing the pan
4 teaspoons unsweetened cocoa powder
1 tablespoon rum
5 tablespoons corn syrup
1 egg white, lightly beaten with 1 tablespoon water
Granulated sugar for sprinkling on top

1. **Making the ganache:** Melt the chocolate over a double boiler or in the microwave on low, until smooth. Remove from heat, add the butter, and stir until incorporated.

2. Stir the cocoa powder into the rum, add the corn syrup, and mix until smooth. Add to the chocolate.

3. **Assembling the brioche:** Lightly butter a 9×4×3-inch nonstick loaf pan. Dust the surface of the refrigerated dough with flour and cut off a 1-pound (grapefruit-size) piece. Dust the piece with more flour and quickly shape it into a ball by stretching the surface of the dough around to the bottom on all four sides, rotating the ball a quarter-turn as you go. Using a rolling pin, roll out the ball into a ¼-inch-thick rectangle, dusting with flour as needed.

4. Spread ½ cup of the ganache evenly over the rectangle, leaving a 1-inch border all around. Starting at the short end, roll up the dough, being careful to seal the bare edges.

5. Gently tuck the loose ends underneath, elongate into an oval, and drop into the prepared pan.

6. Allow to rest 1 hour and 40 minutes.

7. **Twenty minutes before baking time, preheat the oven to 350°F.** If you're not using a stone in the oven, 5 minutes is adequate. Using a pastry brush, paint the top crust with egg white. Sprinkle lightly with granulated sugar.

8. Bake the brioche for about 45 minutes, or until the top is golden brown and the sugar caramelizes. Due to the butter in the dough, the brioche will not form a hard, crackling crust.

9. Remove from the pan and cool slightly; then drizzle the remaining ¼ cup of ganache over the top crust. Cool completely and slice.

Beignets

Beignet is French for fritter, or as we Americans like to call them, dough-nuts. They're made from rich, yeasted dough, fried in oil, and then covered generously in powdered sugar. What's not to love? Here's a re-creation using our simple recipe for this sweet confection, made famous by Café Du Monde in New Orleans.

"My husband and I went to New Orleans for a weekend to eat and listen to jazz. Our first stop in town was Café Du Monde. After two orders of fluffy hot beignets *and plenty of* café au lait, *we were covered in powdered sugar and ready to find some jazz. We managed to return to Café Du Monde at least once every day during our stay. Thank goodness it was largely spared from Hurricane Katrina, so we will be back."*—Zoë

Makes 5 or 6 beignets

Use any of these refrigerated pre-mixed doughs: Challah (page 180) or
   Brioche (page 189)
1 pound (grapefruit-size portion) of either pre-mixed dough shown above,
   defrosted overnight in the refrigerator if frozen
Vegetable oil for deep frying
Powdered sugar

Special Equipment
Deep saucepan for frying, or an electric fryer
Slotted spoon
Paper towels
Candy thermometer

1. Dust the surface of the refrigerated dough with flour and cut off a 1-pound (grapefruit-size) piece. Dust the piece with more flour and quickly shape it into a ball by stretching the surface of the dough around to the bottom on all four sides, rotating the ball a quarter-turn as you go.

2. Roll the dough into a ½-inch-thick rectangle on a lightly floured surface. Using a pizza cutter or knife, cut the dough into 2-inch squares. Allow the dough to rest for 15 to 20 minutes.

3. Meanwhile, fill the saucepan (or electric fryer) with at least 3 inches of oil. Bring the oil to 360 to 370°F as determined by the candy thermometer.

4. Carefully drop the beignets in the hot oil 2 or 3 at a time so they have plenty of room to float to the surface. Do not overcrowd, or they will not rise nicely.

5. After 2 minutes, gently flip the beignets over with a slotted spoon and fry for another minute or until golden brown on both sides.

6. Using the slotted spoon, remove the beignets from the oil and place them on paper towels to drain.

7. Repeat with the remaining dough until all the beignets are fried.

8. Dust generously with powdered sugar and eat with a fresh cup of *café au lait*.

Chocolate- or Jam-Filled Beignets

As if the traditional beignets weren't decadent enough, we felt compelled to fill them with chocolate or jam. They are quite simple to make and everyone who eats them becomes a little bit happier.

Makes 5 or 6 beignets

Use any of these refrigerated pre-mixed doughs: Challah (page 180) or
  Brioche (page 189)
1 pound (grapefruit-size portion) of either pre-mixed dough shown above,
  defrosted overnight in the refrigerator if frozen
Vegetable oil for deep frying
4 ounces semisweet chocolate, cut into ½-ounce pieces, or 4 tablespoons of
  your favorite jam
Powdered sugar

Special Equipment
Deep saucepan for frying, or an electric fryer
Slotted spoon
Paper towels
Candy thermometer

1. Dust the surface of the refrigerated dough with flour and cut off a
   1-pound (grapefruit-size) piece. Dust the piece with more flour and
   quickly shape it into a ball by stretching the surface of the dough around
   to the bottom on all four sides, rotating the ball a quarter-turn as you go.

2. Roll the dough into a ¼-inch-thick rectangle on a lightly floured surface.
   Using a pizza cutter or knife, cut the dough into 2-inch squares, then
   place a half-ounce of chocolate or a teaspoon of jam in the center of
   each square. Gather the edges of the dough around the filling, pinching
   at the center to form a seal. If you are not able to seal the edges *very*
   well, use a small amount of water to help stick them together.

3. Allow the beignets to rest for 15 to 20 minutes while the oil heats up to 360 to 370°F as determined by the candy thermometer.

4. Carefully drop the beignets in the hot oil, 2 or 3 at a time so they have plenty of room to rise to the surface. Do not overcrowd or they will not rise nicely.

5. After 2 minutes, gently flip the beignets over with a slotted spoon and fry for another minute or until golden brown on both sides.

6. Using the slotted spoon, remove the beignets from the oil and drain on paper towels. Repeat with the remaining dough until all the beignets are fried.

7. Dust generously with powdered sugar and eat with a fresh cup of *café au lait*.

Panettone

Panettone is the classic Christmas bread sold all over Italy during the holidays. It finds its origins in Milan around the fifteenth century, and has been the subject of much lore. The most often told story of how this bejeweled bread came to be goes something like this: A young nobleman falls in love with a baker's daughter named Toni. The nobleman disguises himself as a pastry chef's apprentice and creates the tall fruit-studded bread to present to Toni, calling it *"Pan de Toni."* The bread is a success in the bakery and the father blesses the marriage.

The story is rich and fanciful, just like the bread, made with dried fruit and the essence of lemons and vanilla. There are traditional *panettone* molds that are very high sided and come either straight or fluted. They can be found at cooking stores or on the Web. You can use a brioche mold, but the bread won't have the classic high sides. Paper *panettone* molds are available from baking supply stores.

Makes three 1½-pound loaves. The recipe is easily doubled or halved.

1½ cups lukewarm water

1½ tablespoons granulated yeast (1½ packets)

1½ tablespoons salt

½ cup honey

8 eggs, lightly beaten

1 cup (2 sticks) unsalted butter, melted, plus more for greasing the pan

1 teaspoon lemon extract

2 teaspoons vanilla extract

2 teaspoons lemon zest

7½ cups unbleached all-purpose flour

2 cups mixed dried and/or candied fruit, chopped (golden raisins, dried pineapple, dried apricots, dried cherries, and candied citrus, just to name a few that we've tried and loved in this bread)

Egg wash (1 egg beaten with 1 tablespoon of water)

1. **Mixing and storing the dough:** Mix the yeast, salt, honey, eggs, melted butter, extracts, and zest with the water in a 5-quart bowl, or a lidded (not airtight) food container.

2. Mix in the flour and dried fruit without kneading, using a spoon, a 14-cup capacity food processor (with dough attachment), or a heavy-duty stand mixer (with dough hook). If you're not using a machine, you may need to use wet hands to incorporate the last bit of flour. The dough will be loose, but will firm up when chilled (don't try to use it without chilling).

3. Cover (not airtight), and allow to rest at room temperature until the dough rises and collapses (or flattens on top), approximately 2 hours.

4. The dough can be used as soon as it's chilled after the initial rise, or frozen for later use. Refrigerate in a lidded (not airtight) container and use over the next 5 days. Beyond that, freeze the dough in 1-pound portions in an airtight container up to 4 weeks. When using frozen dough, thaw in the refrigerator for 24 hours before using, then allow the usual rest and rise time.

5. **On baking day,** grease a *panettone* or brioche pan with a small amount of butter.

6. Dust the surface of the refrigerated dough with flour and cut off a 1½-pound (cantaloupe-size) piece. Dust the piece with more flour and quickly shape it into a ball by stretching the surface of the dough around to the bottom on all four sides, rotating the ball a quarter-turn as you go. Place the ball into the pan, seam side down.

7. Loosely cover the dough with oiled plastic wrap and allow to rest at room temperature for 1 hour and 40 minutes.

8. **Twenty minutes before baking time, preheat the oven to 375°F.** The baking stone is not essential for loaf pan breads; if you omit it the preheat may be as short as 5 minutes.

9. Remove the plastic wrap and brush the *panettone* with egg wash. Bake in the center of the oven without steam for 50 to 55 minutes, or until golden brown and hollow sounding when tapped. The amount of dough and baking times will vary depending on the pan size.

10. Allow to cool before slicing or eating.

Soft American-Style White Bread

American-style sliced white bread doesn't get a lot of respect from serious bread lovers. Most of our experience with it is based on plastic-wrapped products, often chemically preserved on the shelf for long periods of time. But it doesn't have to be this way. With this recipe you can produce something much nicer.

While many people will be happy with the Crusty White Sandwich Loaf in Chapter 5, some kids will want a bread with a softer crust. What they're hankering for is the shortening—that's what keeps commercial crusts so soft. We chose to use plain old creamery butter in ours, and a little sugar for tenderness. Try it with our grilled *Croque Monsieur* French ham and cheese sandwich (page 206).

Makes three 1½-pound loaves. The recipe is easily doubled or halved.

3 cups lukewarm water
1½ tablespoons granulated yeast (1½ packets)
1½ tablespoons salt
2 tablespoons sugar
½ cup (1 stick) unsalted butter, melted, plus additional for brushing the top
    crust
7 cups unbleached all-purpose flour
Neutral-tasting oil or softened butter for greasing baking pan

1. **Mixing and storing the dough:** Mix the yeast, salt, sugar, and melted butter with the water in a 5-quart bowl, or a lidded (not airtight) food container.

2. Mix in the flour without kneading, using a spoon, a 14-cup capacity food processor (with dough attachment), or a heavy-duty stand mixer (with dough hook). If you're not using a machine, you may need to use wet hands to incorporate the last bit of flour.

3. Cover (not airtight), and allow to rest at room temperature until the dough rises and collapses (or flattens on top), approximately 2 hours.

4. The dough can be used immediately after the initial rise with only a 40-minute rest in the pan, though it is easier to handle when cold. Refrigerate the remaining dough in a lidded (not airtight) container and use over the next 7 days.

5. **On baking day,** lightly grease a 9×4×3-inch nonstick loaf pan. Dust the surface of the refrigerated dough with flour and cut off a 1½-pound (cantaloupe-size) piece. Dust the piece with more flour and quickly shape it into a ball by stretching the surface of the dough around to the bottom on all four sides, rotating the ball a quarter-turn as you go. Elongate the ball into an oval.

6. Drop the dough into the prepared pan. You want to fill the pan slightly more than half-full.

7. Allow the dough to rest for 1 hour and 40 minutes (or just 40 minutes if you're using fresh, unrefrigerated dough). Dust the loaf with flour and slash the top, using the tip of a sharp knife. Brush the top surface with melted butter.

8. **Twenty minutes before baking time, preheat the oven to 350°F.** If you're not using a stone in the oven, 5 minutes is adequate. A baking stone is not essential when using a loaf pan.

9. Bake the bread near the center of the oven for about 45 minutes, or until golden brown.

10. Allow to cool completely before slicing, or it will be nearly impossible to achieve reasonable sandwich slices.

Croque Monsieur

This classic Parisian street food is a hearty and simple sandwich. Start with freshly baked sandwich bread, slather it with Dijon mayonnaise, add some Gruyère cheese and ham, and then grill it in butter. Serve it with a glass of light red wine and a salad for a little bit of heaven.

Makes 1 sandwich

1½ tablespoons mayonnaise
2 teaspoons whole-grain Dijon mustard
2 slices sandwich loaf bread (page 204)
1 teaspoon butter, plus more if needed
1½ ounces Gruyère cheese
2 ounces thinly sliced ham

1. Blend together the mayonnaise and mustard; set aside.

2. Butter one side of each slice of bread, and spread the other side with the mustard-mayonnaise mixture. Place one slice of bread, butter-side down, in a skillet.

3. Cover with half the cheese, then the ham. Finish with the other half of the cheese.

4. Place the skillet over medium-low heat and grill slowly for approximately 4 minutes per side, or until browned and crisp. Add additional butter to the pan if needed.

Buttermilk Bread

Many traditional American and British breads use buttermilk, which tenderizes the bread, creating a lovely soft crust and crumb, and a terrific flavor. It makes an ideal sandwich loaf, and it's heavenly in Judy's Board of Directors' Cinnamon-Raisin Bread (page 209). You can also use this dough in place of any of the Boule dough recipes in Chapter 5, lowering the baking temperature to 375°F.

Makes three 1½-pound loaves. The recipe is easily doubled or halved.

2 cups lukewarm water
1 cup buttermilk
1½ tablespoons granulated yeast (1½ packets)
1½ tablespoons salt
1½ tablespoons sugar
6½ cups unbleached all-purpose flour
Butter or neutral-tasting oil for greasing the pan

1. **Mixing and storing the dough:** Mix the yeast, salt, and sugar with the water and buttermilk in a 5-quart bowl, or a lidded (not airtight) food container.

2. Mix in the flour without kneading, using a spoon, a 14-cup capacity food processor (with dough attachment), or a heavy-duty stand mixer (with dough hook). If you're not using a machine, you may need to use wet hands to incorporate the last bit of flour.

3. Cover (not airtight), and allow to rest at room temperature until the dough rises and collapses (or flattens on top), approximately 2 hours.

4. The dough can be used immediately after the initial rise, though it is easier to handle when cold. Refrigerate in a lidded (not airtight) container and use over the next 7 days.

5. **On baking day,** lightly grease a 9×4×3-inch nonstick loaf pan. Dust the surface of the refrigerated dough with flour and cut off a 1½-pound (cantaloupe-size) piece. Dust the piece with more flour and quickly shape it into a ball by stretching the surface of the dough around to the bottom on all four sides, rotating the ball a quarter-turn as you go. Elongate the ball into an oval.

6. Drop the dough into the prepared pan. You want to fill the pan slightly more than half-full.

7. Allow the dough to rest for 1 hour and 40 minutes (or just 40 minutes if you're using fresh, unrefrigerated dough). Dust the loaf with flour and slash the top, using the tip of a sharp knife. Brush the top surface with melted butter.

8. **Twenty minutes before baking time, preheat the oven to 350°F.** If you're not using a stone in the oven, 5 minutes is adequate. A baking stone is not essential when using a loaf pan.

9. Bake the bread near the center of the oven for about 45 minutes, or until golden brown.

10. Remove from the pan. Allow to cool completely before slicing, or it will be nearly impossible to achieve reasonable sandwich slices.

Judy's Board of Directors' Cinnamon-Raisin Bread

"My friend Judy is the C.E.O. of a successful company. She has a passion for bread that she brings into the boardroom. At one tense meeting with her Board of Directors, she used the simple magic of shaping loaves to win over skeptical board members. She slammed the dough onto the conference table.

"'Growing a company,' Judy told them, 'is like baking bread. Sometimes you have to be patient, and wait for the dough to rise. You can't rush it. Things need to develop spontaneously, on their own.'

"She shaped a loaf, pushing and prodding. The loaf was formed—cinnamon-raisin bread! And the Board gave its blessing to the company's next stage. She's continued to serve this bread, with butter and jam, at all kinds of business meetings, tense or otherwise."—Jeff

We've adapted Judy's recipe for our quick method. As always with our dough, don't bother kneading (unless you're trying to intimidate your Board).

Makes three 1½-pound loaves. The recipe is easily doubled or halved.

1½ pounds (cantaloupe-size portion) Buttermilk Bread dough (page 207)
Butter or neutral-tasting oil for greasing the pan
1½ teaspoons ground cinnamon
⅓ cup sugar
¾ cup raisins
Egg wash (1 egg beaten with 1 tablespoon water)

1. Lightly grease a 9×4×3-inch nonstick loaf pan. Set aside. Dust the surface of the refrigerated dough with flour and cut off a 1½-pound (cantaloupe-size) piece. Dust the piece with more flour and quickly shape it into a ball by stretching the surface of the dough around to the bottom on all four sides, rotating the ball a quarter-turn as you go.

2. With a rolling pin, roll out the dough to an 8×16-inch rectangle about ¼-inch thick, dusting the board and rolling pan with flour as needed. You may need to use a metal dough scraper to loosen rolled dough from the board as you are working with it.

3. Using a pastry brush, cover the surface of the dough lightly with egg wash. Mix together the sugar and cinnamon and sprinkle the mixture evenly over the dough. Evenly distribute the raisins.

4. Starting from the short side, roll it up jelly-roll style. Pinch the edges and ends together, tucking the ends under.

5. Place the loaf seam side down in the prepared pan. Allow to rest 1 hour and 40 minutes (or just 40 minutes if you're using fresh, unrefrigerated dough).

6. **Twenty minutes before baking time, preheat the oven to 375°F.** If you're not using a stone in the oven, 5 minutes is adequate. The stone is not essential when using a loaf pan.

7. Bake for 35 to 40 minutes, or until golden brown.

8. Remove from pan and allow to cool before slicing.

Chocolate Bread

Chocolate bread is found in artisan bakeries all over the country. Its origin is unknown, but we'd like to thank the chocophile who found yet another way to satisfy our chocolate cravings. The honey is subtle, allowing chocolate's bittersweet notes to come through. It's not chocolate cake; it's better, and much less ordinary. The texture says bread, but chocolate cake lovers won't be disappointed. Door County Sour Cherry Preserves (page 213) is a perfect not-too-sweet counterpoint here.

Makes two 1½-pound loaves. The recipe is easily doubled or halved.

4 ounces premium bittersweet chocolate, preferably Valrhona or equivalent
½ cup unsalted butter
1¾ cups lukewarm water
1½ tablespoons granulated yeast (or 1½ packets)
1½ tablespoons salt
4 large eggs, lightly beaten
⅔ cup honey
5½ cups unbleached all-purpose flour
1 cup premium unsweetened cocoa powder, preferably Valrhona or equivalent
5 ounces finely chopped bittersweet chocolate, preferably Valrhona or equivalent
Butter or neutral-tasting oil for greasing the cookie sheet

1. **Making the ganache:** Melt the 4 ounces of chocolate and the butter in a double-boiler or microwave until chocolate is melted. Blend together and set aside.

2. **Mixing and storing the dough:** Mix the yeast, salt, eggs, and honey with the water in a 5-quart bowl, or a lidded (not airtight) food container.

3. Mix in the flour, cocoa powder, ganache, and the 5 ounces of chocolate without kneading, using a spoon, a 14-cup capacity food processor (with dough attachment), or a heavy-duty stand mixer (with dough

hook). If you're not using a machine, you may need to use wet hands to incorporate the last bit of flour.

4.   Cover (not airtight), and allow to rest at room temperature until the dough rises and collapses (or flattens on top), approximately 2 hours.

5.   The dough can be used immediately after the initial rise, though it is easier to handle when cold. Refrigerate in a lidded (not airtight) container and use over the next 5 days. Beyond 5 days, freeze the dough in 1-pound portions in an airtight container for up to 4 weeks. When using frozen dough, thaw in the refrigerator for 24 hours before using, then allow the usual rest and rise time.

6.   **On baking day,** line a cookie sheet with parchment paper or a silicone mat. Dust the surface of the refrigerated dough with flour and cut off a 1½-pound (canteloupe-size) piece. Dust the piece with more flour and quickly shape it into a ball by stretching the surface of the dough around to the bottom on all four sides, rotating the ball a quarter-turn as you go.

7.   Allow the ball to rest and rise on the prepared cookie sheet for 1 hour and 40 minutes (or just 40 minutes if you're using fresh, unrefrigerated dough). Paint with egg wash.

8.   **Twenty minutes before baking time, preheat the oven to 350°F.** If you're not using a stone in the oven, 5 minutes is adequate. The stone is not essential when using a cookie sheet.

9.   Place the bread in the center of the oven and bake for about 35 minutes. Smaller or larger loaves will require adjustments in baking time.

10. Remove from pan. Allow to cool before slicing or eating.

Door County Sour Cherry Preserves

Door County in Wisconsin produces some of the world's most flavorful sour cherries. If you can get there in late July or early August you'll find them at their peak of perfection. Pick them yourself, or buy fresh from a farm stand, but choose the Montmorency variety if they're available. They are quite tart, but their explosive and spicy fruit flavor is brought out by the sugar in the preserve. This is a fantastic combination with Chocolate Bread (page 211). As in Laura's Three-Citrus Marmalade (page 96), the Sure-Jell box was the culinary inspiration.

If you're intimidated by canning, make a smaller quantity and simply skip the sterilization procedure in the final step, then refrigerate the preserves for up to 2 months or freeze them for up to a year.

Makes 6 cups

3 pounds ripe sour cherries (Montmorency variety if available), or enough to
    make 4 cups when pitted and finely chopped
1 box (1.75 ounces) Sure-Jell fruit pectin
4¾ cups sugar

1. Measure the sugar and set aside. Do not be tempted to reduce the amount of sugar, or the preserves may not set properly.

2. Remove the stems from the cherries and pit them (a cherry pitter is helpful here). Chop the cherries finely, and measure exactly 4 cups.

3. Place the measured cherries and their juice into a 6- to 8-quart saucepan. Stir in the box of fruit pectin and bring the mixture to a full rolling boil.

4. Stir in the sugar quickly, return to a full rolling boil, and cook for 1 minute. Remove from heat and skim off any foam.

5. Pour the preserves into clean canning jars. Process according to canner
    and U.S. Department of Agriculture instructions, or refrigerate and use
    within 2 months. The preserves also can be frozen, without canning,
    for up to 1 year.

Swiss Muesli Breakfast Bread

This dough will be wet and sticky when you are mixing it, but will be easier to handle once you refrigerate it. And it bakes up with a glorious moist texture. The final result makes for a hearty breakfast bread, which is slightly sweet and wonderful with preserves.

Makes one 1½-pound loaf

1½-pound (cantaloupe-size portion) Challah (page 180) or Brioche dough
   (page 189), defrosted overnight in the refrigerator if frozen
¾ cup Swiss muesli
½ cup milk
Egg wash (1 egg beaten with 1 tablespoon of water)
Whole wheat flour for the pizza peel

1. **On baking day,** mix together the Swiss muesli and the milk and allow to stand for 10 minutes.

2. Dust the surface of the refrigerated dough with flour and cut off a 1½-pound (cantaloupe-size) piece. Place it into a bowl. Using your hands, blend the muesli into the dough; this will be reminiscent of making mud pies!

3. Dust the piece with more flour and quickly shape it into a ball by stretching the surface of the dough around to the bottom on all four sides, rotating the ball a quarter-turn as you go.

4. Allow the ball to rest for 1 hour and 40 minutes on a flour-covered pizza peel (or just 40 minutes if you're using fresh, unrefrigerated dough).

5. Using a pastry brush, brush the top crust with egg wash.

6. **Twenty minutes before baking time, preheat the oven to 350°F,** with a baking stone placed on a middle rack.

7. Bake the loaf directly on the stone without steam for about 30 minutes until golden brown. Due to the fat in the dough, the bread will not form a hard, crackling crust.

8. Allow to cool before slicing or eating.

Sunflower Seed Breakfast Loaf

"Thomas Gumpel, my bread instructor and friend from the Culinary Institute of America, inspired this recipe. The first time I made the bread in his class was under some duress. I'd been a bit impertinent during a lecture and he decided to make an example of my kitchen misdemeanor. He had me mix the sunflower bread in an old-fashioned 'bread bucket' (circa 1900) in the dining hall as public humiliation. The process took the better part of the class period, and my pride, albeit strong, took some abuse. But the bread was sublime. As harrowing as my first experience with this bread was, I've always loved to make it, but now it takes only a fraction of the time to prepare."—Zoë

Makes three 1½-pound loaves. The recipe is easily doubled or halved.

2 cups lukewarm milk
½ cup honey
2 tablespoons sugar
1½ tablespoons salt
1½ tablespoons granulated yeast (1½ packets)
4 tablespoons sunflower oil (or canola oil), plus more for greasing the pan
3 eggs
6 cups bread flour
1 cup sunflower seeds

1. **Mixing and storing the dough:** Mix the honey, sugar, salt, yeast, sunflower oil, and eggs with the lukewarm milk in a 5-quart bowl, or a lidded (not airtight) food container.

2. Mix in the flour without kneading, using a spoon, a 14-cup capacity food processor (with dough attachment), or a heavy-duty stand mixer (with dough hook). If you're not using a machine, you may need to use wet hands to incorporate the last bit of flour. Add the 1 cup of sunflower seeds to the dough.

3. Cover (not airtight), and allow to rest at room temperature until the dough rises and collapses (or flattens on top), approximately 2 hours.

4. The dough can be used immediately after the initial rise, though it is easier to handle when cold. Refrigerate in a lidded (not airtight) container and use over the next 9 days.

5. **On baking day,** Lightly grease a 9×4×3-inch nonstick loaf pan. Cut off and form a 1½-pound cylinder and place in the pan. Allow to rest and rise for 1 hour and 40 minutes (or just 40 minutes if you're using fresh, unrefrigerated dough).

6. **Twenty minutes before baking time, preheat the oven to 375°F.** The baking stone is not essential for loaf pan breads; if you omit it the pre-heat may be as short as 5 minutes.

7. Place the bread in the center of the oven and bake for 35 to 40 minutes, without steam, or until golden brown.

8. Remove from pan and allow to cool before slicing or eating.

Chocolate Prune Bread

This bread is a great combination of flavors; it is rich and powerfully chocolatey (especially if you use chocolate dough as the base) without being too sweet. We like to use bittersweet chocolate, but semisweet will work beautifully as well.

Some years ago, the National Prune Council decided that prunes had a public relations problem, so these days the fruit is known as "dried plum" rather than prune. We're sticking with "prunes." Whatever the name they're delicious, nutritious, and have a marvelous concentrated flavor that says, well, prunes. This bread pairs well with a glass of Armagnac (or a glass of milk!)

Makes one 1½-pound loaf

Use any of these refrigerated pre-mixed doughs: Challah dough (page 180), Brioche dough (page 189), or Chocolate Bread dough (page 211)
1½ pounds (cantaloupe-size portion) of any pre-mixed dough listed above
Softened butter for greasing the pan
6 ounces chopped high-quality bittersweet chocolate (2 ounces if using Chocolate Bread dough), preferably Valrhona or equivalent
¾ cup chopped prunes
Egg wash (1 egg beaten with 1 tablespoon of water)
4 tablespoons sugar for sprinkling over the top of the bread and preparing the pan

1. **On baking day,** generously grease a 9×4×3-inch nonstick loaf pan with butter, sprinkle sugar evenly over the butter, and shake the pan to distribute.

2. Dust the surface of the refrigerated dough with flour and cut off a 1½-pound (cantaloupe-size) piece. Dust the piece with more flour and quickly shape it into a ball by stretching the surface of the dough around to the bottom on all four sides, rotating the ball a quarter-turn

as you go. Using a rolling pin, roll out the dough into a ½-inch-thick rectangle. As you roll out the dough, use enough flour to prevent it from sticking to the work surface but not so much as to make the dough dry.

3. Sprinkle the chocolate and chopped prunes over the dough and roll the dough up to encase them. Fold the dough over itself several times, turning and pressing it down with the heel of your hand after each turn. This will work the chocolate and prunes into the dough; some may poke through.

4. With very wet hands, form the dough into a loaf shape and place it in the prepared pan. Cover loosely with plastic wrap and allow to rest and rise for 1 hour and 40 minutes (or just 40 minutes if you're using fresh, unrefrigerated dough).

5. **Twenty minutes before baking time, preheat the oven to 350°F.** The baking stone is not essential for loaf pan breads; if you omit it, the preheat may be as short as 5 minutes. Just before putting the bread in the oven brush the top with egg wash and sprinkle with sugar.

6. Bake the loaf in the center of the oven, without steam, for 40 to 50 minutes, or until firm. Smaller or larger loaves will require adjustments in baking time.

7. Remove from pan. Allow to cool before slicing or eating.

Chocolate-Raisin Babka

In our *babka*, based on a Ukrainian recipe, we call for 16 egg yolks, which make it extremely rich and velvety. In the traditional method, the milk and flour are cooked together, and the egg yolks are added one by one— sometimes up to 30 of them! We've simplified the recipe without losing any of the old-fashioned charm. You can freeze the leftover egg whites and use them later to make meringue.

Makes four 1-pound loaves. The recipe is easily doubled or halved.

3 cups lukewarm milk
16 egg yolks
2 tablespoons granulated yeast (1½ packets)
½ cup sugar
2 teaspoon salt
12 tablespoons melted unsalted butter, plus more for greasing the pan
7½ cups all-purpose flour
¾ cup raisins
¾ cup finely chopped or shaved bittersweet chocolate
¼ cup rum for soaking the baked loaf

1. **Mixing and storing the dough:** Mix the egg yolks, yeast, sugar, salt, and melted butter with the milk in a 5-quart bowl, or a lidded (not airtight) food container.

2. Mix in the flour without kneading, using a spoon, a 14-cup capacity food processor (with dough attachment), or a heavy-duty stand mixer (with dough hook). The mixture will be quite loose because of all the yolks.

3. Cover (not airtight), and allow to rest at room temperature until the dough rises and collapses (or flattens on top), approximately 2 hours. Brush rum onto loaf when slightly cooled.

4. Due to all the egg yolks, you must chill the dough before using it. Refrigerate in a lidded (not airtight) container and use over the next 5 days. Beyond five days, freeze the dough in 1-pound portions in an airtight container for up to four weeks. When using frozen dough, thaw in refrigerator for 24 hours before use, then allow the usual rest and rise times.

5. **On baking day,** grease a *babka*, bundt, or nonstick loaf pan. Dust the surface of the refrigerated dough with flour and cut off a 1-pound (grapefruit-size) piece. Dust the piece with more flour and quickly shape it into a ball by stretching the surface of the dough around to the bottom on all four sides, rotating the ball a quarter-turn as you go.

6. Using a rolling pin, roll the dough into a ¼-inch-thick rectangle. Sprinkle the raisins and chocolate evenly over the dough. Roll the dough into a log, starting at the short end. Fold the dough so the two ends meet and form it into a ball.

7. Fill the pan with dough so it is approximately two-thirds full. Allow to rest and rise 1 hour and 40 minutes (or just 40 minutes if you're using fresh, unrefrigerated dough).

8. **Twenty minutes before baking time, preheat the oven to 350°F.** The baking stone is not essential for loaf pan breads; if you omit it, the preheat can be as short as 5 minutes.

9. Place the pan near the center of the oven (not directly on the stone if you're using one). Bake for about 35 minutes, or until golden brown and firm.

10. Allow to cool before slicing or eating.

Apple and Pear Coffee Cake

"Every year our family goes to the orchards to pick apples. Here in Min-nesota we are blessed with the finest apples I've ever experienced. I like to bake with a combination; some sweet and some tart, some that keep their shape and some that will break down and get saucy. No matter what apple you pick, this recipe will be a favorite. I like to include the pear for the variety of flavor, adding almost a perfumey quality."—Zoë

Makes 1 coffee cake

The Streusel Topping
1 cup oats
1 cup all-purpose flour
1 cup brown sugar
1 cup chopped nuts, optional
½ cup melted butter
Pinch of ground cinnamon

The Cake
1½ pounds (cantaloupe-size portion) Brioche dough (page 189)
Butter for greasing the pan
2 small apples, 1 tart and 1 sweet, thinly sliced
1 Bosc pear, thinly sliced
3 tablespoons brown sugar
Zest of half an orange
1½ cups streusel topping (above)

1. **Prepare the topping:** Combine all streusel ingredients in a bowl and mix until the butter is roughly incorporated. Don't overmix—you want a crumbly texture. Set aside.

2. **Assembling the cake:** Grease an 8-inch cake pan with butter and dust with flour. Set aside.

3. Toss the apples, pear, brown sugar, and zest together in a small bowl and set aside.

4. Dust the surface of the refrigerated dough with flour and cut off a cantaloupe-size piece. Dust with more flour and quickly shape it into a rough ball by stretching the surface of the dough around to the bottom on all four sides, rotating the ball a quarter-turn as you go.

5. Roll out the dough into a ⅛-inch-thick rectangle, approximately 12×16 inches. As you roll out the dough, add flour as needed to prevent sticking.

6. Cut the dough into two 8-inch rounds, by tracing the bottom of the cake pan. Save any scraps for Cinnamon Twists and Turns (page 233).

7. Place one of the dough rounds in the bottom of the prepared cake pan. Top with half the apple mixture and then sprinkle half the streusel topping over it. Repeat with next layer of dough, apple mixture, and streusel.

8. Rest the cake for 1 hour and 20 minutes.

9. **Twenty minutes before baking time, preheat the oven to 375°F.** The baking stone is not essential for pan breads; if you omit it the preheat can be as short as 5 minutes.

10. Bake the cake in the center of the oven about 45 minutes, or until a skewer inserted in the center comes out clean.

11. Allow to cool for 10 to 15 minutes. While the cake is still warm, place a plate over the top and invert the cake out of the pan onto the plate. Cover with a serving plate and invert again.

12. Serve warm or at room temperature with whipped cream, or just on its own.

Sunny-Side-Up Apricot Pastry

It's as fun to make and look at as it is to eat. This combination of buttery brioche dough, sweet vanilla pastry cream, and tart apricots masquerading as a sunny-side-up egg was made popular in Julia Child's book *Baking with Julia*.

Pastry cream is a staple in the pastry kitchen. To flavor this silky custard, you can use pure vanilla extract, or try a vanilla bean, which gives the most intense and satisfying flavor. If you have never had the opportunity to cook with a real vanilla bean, try it now and you'll be hooked. To use the bean, just slice it lengthwise with a paring knife to expose the seeds. Scrape the seeds out of the pod and throw the seeds and the pod into your saucepan. The pod will get strained out at the end, leaving the fragrant aroma and the flecks of real vanilla behind.

Makes eight 4-inch pastries

The Pastry Cream
2 cups milk
½ cup sugar
2 tablespoons unsalted butter
Pinch of salt
½ vanilla bean or 1 teaspoon pure vanilla extract
3 tablespoons cornstarch
1 egg
3 egg yolks

The Pastries
1½ pounds (cantaloupe-size portion) Brioche dough (page 189)
1 cup pastry cream (above)
8 ripe apricots, halved (fresh in season or canned)
½ cup apricot jam, melted
2 cups sugar

For the Pastry Cream

1. Bring the milk, ¼ cup of the sugar, butter, salt, and vanilla bean to a gentle boil in a medium to large saucepan. Remove from the heat.

2. Whisk together the cornstarch and the remaining ¼ cup of sugar. Add the egg and egg yolks to the cornstarch and mix into a smooth paste.

3. Slowly, and in small amounts, whisk a little of the hot milk into the egg mixture. Once the egg mixture is warm to the touch, pour it back into the milk in the pan.

4. Return the custard to the stove and bring to a boil, whisking continuously for 2 to 3 minutes until thickened.

5. Strain the pastry cream into a shallow container and cover with plastic wrap pressed directly on the surface to keep a skin from forming.

6. Set the container in the freezer for 15 minutes, then refrigerate.

For the Pastries

7. Line a cookie sheet with parchment paper or a silicone mat.

8. Dust the surface of the refrigerated dough with flour and cut off a cantaloupe-size piece. Dust the piece with more flour and quickly shape it into a rough ball by stretching the surface of the dough around to the bottom on all four sides, rotating the ball a quarter-turn as you go.

9. Roll the dough to a ⅛-inch thick rectangle, adding flour as needed to prevent sticking.

10. Cut out eight 4-inch circles, using a round cookie cutter. Save the scraps to use in Cinnamon Twists and Turns (page 233).

11. Cover the work surface with a generous coating of the sugar. Take one of the 4 rounds and lay it in the sugar. Using a rolling pin, roll back and forth over the center, stopping ½ inch from the two ends to create an oval. If the dough sticks to the rolling pin, dust the pin with a bit of flour. Lay the oval, sugar side up, on the lined cookie sheet. Repeat with the rest of the dough, keeping the ovals at least 1 inch apart on the sheet.

12. Spread 2 tablespoons of the pastry cream in the center of each sugared oval. Place 2 apricots over the pastry cream so they resemble sunny-side-up eggs. Rest the pastry for 45 minutes.

13. **Twenty minutes before baking time, preheat the oven to 375°F.** If you're not using a stone in the oven, 5 minutes is adequate. The stone is not essential when using a cookie sheet.

14. Bake the pastries in the center of the oven for about 35 minutes, or until the dough is golden brown and the sugar is nicely caramelized.

15. As soon as the pastries come out of the oven, brush the apricot jam over the apricots to give them a nice shine. Serve warm or cooled.

Blueberry Lemon Curd Ring

This wreath-shaped pastry showcases the bright flavors of fresh lemon and the sweetness of in-season blueberries.

The delicious lemon curd is perfect for slathering on a hot piece of toast as well as for the filling of this pastry recipe.

Makes 1

The Lemon Curd
6 egg yolks
1 cup sugar
½ cup lemon juice
1 tablespoon lemon zest
1 stick unsalted butter, cut into ½-inch slices

The Ring
1½ pounds (cantaloupe-size portion) Brioche dough (page 189)
½ cup lemon curd
2 tablespoons sugar
1½ cups fresh blueberries
Egg wash (1 egg beaten with 1 tablespoon of water)
Sugar for dusting the top

For the Lemon Curd

1. Whisk together all the ingredients except the butter in a large metal bowl.

2. Place the bowl over a pot of gently simmering water set up as a double boiler.

3. Stir constantly with a rubber spatula until the lemon curd begins to thicken, about 10 minutes.

4. Add the butter and continue to stir until it is completely melted and the curd is quite thick; it will be the consistency of smooth pudding.

5. If there are any lumps, strain the curd into a container; then cover with plastic wrap and place in the freezer until cool. Then refrigerate.

For the Ring

6. Line a cookie sheet with parchment paper or a silicone mat.

7. Dust the surface of the refrigerated dough with flour and cut off a cantaloupe-size piece. Dust the piece with more flour and quickly shape it into a ball by stretching the surface of the dough around to the bottom on all four sides, rotating the ball a quarter-turn as you go.

8. Roll out the ball to a $1/8$-inch-thick rectangle approximately 12×16 inches. As you roll out the dough, add flour as needed to prevent sticking.

9. Spread the lemon curd evenly over the dough. Sprinkle the berries over the lemon curd.

10. Starting with the long side of the dough, roll it up into a log. Join the two ends together to form a wreath shape; pinch together to seal. Place on the prepared cookie sheet. Stretch the dough to make sure you have a nice wide opening in the middle of your wreath.

11. Make evenly spaced cuts all the way around the wreath about $1\frac{1}{2}$ to 2 inches apart. The cuts should go nearly to the bottom of the dough but not all the way through, about $\frac{1}{2}$ inch from the bottom of the log.

12. Fold every other cut piece out away from the center. Allow the dough to rest for about 40 minutes.

13. **Preheat the oven to 375°F.** Brush the dough with egg wash and generously dust with sugar.

14. Bake the ring in the center of the oven for 35 to 40 minutes, or until golden brown and well set. Serve warm or cooled.

Braided Raspberry Almond Cream Pastry

Although this is easy to put together, the end result is dramatic and impressive for a special brunch or potluck. If fresh raspberries are unavailable, it's a wonderful way to show off seasonal fruits like apples, pears, peaches, and cherries.

Makes 1

1½ pounds (cantaloupe-size portion) Brioche dough (page 189)
½ cup almond cream (page 193)
½ cup raspberry jam
1 cup fresh raspberries
Egg wash (1 egg beaten with 1 tablespoon of water)
Sugar for dusting the top

1. Line a cookie sheet with parchment paper or a silicone mat.

2. Dust the surface of the refrigerated dough with flour and cut off a cantaloupe-size piece. Dust the piece with more flour and quickly shape it into a ball by stretching the surface of the dough around to the bottom on all four sides, rotating the ball a quarter-turn as you go.

3. Roll out the dough into a ⅛-inch-thick rectangle. As you roll out the dough, add flour as needed to prevent sticking.

4. Lift the dough onto the lined cookie sheet. Cover the center third of the dough with the almond cream, the jam, and the berries.

5. Using a pizza cutter, cut about twelve ½-inch-wide strips down each side. Brush the strips lightly with egg wash. Fold the strips, left over right, crisscrossing over the filling (see photo, page 232). Lightly press the strips together as you move down the pastry, creating a braid. Allow the braid to rest for 40 minutes.

6. **Preheat the oven to 375°F.** Brush the braid with egg wash and generously sprinkle with sugar.

7. Place the cookie sheet in the center of the oven. Bake the braid for 35 to 45 minutes, or until golden brown and bubbling. Serve warm.

Cinnamon Twists and Turns

This is a great recipe for leftover scraps of rolled-out Brioche dough. The end result may look a bit like modern art, but the flavor will be a real treat— wonderful with a cup of coffee.

½ cup sugar
1 tablespoon cinnamon
Brioche dough or scraps
Egg wash (1 egg beaten with 1 tablespoon of water)

1. Line a cookie sheet with parchment paper or a silicone mat.

2. **Preheat the oven to 375°F.** If you're not using a stone in the oven, 5 minutes is adequate. The stone is not essential when using a cookie sheet.

3. Mix the sugar and cinnamon together in a small bowl. Set aside.

4. Brush the surface of the brioche scraps very lightly with egg wash, and sprinkle generously with the cinnamon-sugar. Flip the dough over and repeat on the opposite side.

5. Using a pizza cutter, cut the dough into ¾-inch strips or leave the scraps in odd shapes. Twist the strips into spirals and space evenly on the cookie sheet. Let rest for 15 minutes. Depending on the size of the twists, they may turn in the oven and take on their own shape.

6. Bake for 15 to 20 minutes, or until golden brown. Serve warm.

Bread Pudding

Bread pudding is the ultimate comfort food. It is also the perfect use for the day-old bread you will have left over when making all the recipes in this book. We like to use slightly stale bread because it absorbs the custard so well. This is wonderful served with Kumquat Champagne Confit (recipe follows) when you want something decadent for brunch.

Makes 8 servings

8 egg yolks
1 cup sugar
1 quart half-and-half
¼ cup rum or brandy (optional)
1 teaspoon vanilla
¼ teaspoon freshly grated nutmeg
¼ teaspoon cinnamon
½ teaspoon freshly grated orange zest
12 slices day-old bread, cut ½ inch thick
¾ cup raisins, optional

1. **Preheat the oven to 325°F.**

2. In a large mixing bowl, whisk together the yolks, sugar, half-and-half, rum, vanilla, nutmeg, cinnamon, and zest until well combined.

3. Arrange the bread slices to fit nicely in an 8×12×2-inch baking dish. Sprinkle the raisins over the bread if using. Pour the custard slowly over the bread; let sit about 10 minutes. You may have to push the bread into the custard to guarantee no bread remains dry.

4. Cover loosely with foil, poking a few holes in the top to allow steam to escape. Place on the center rack. Bake for 1 hour, or until the center is just firm.

5. Remove from the oven and allow to stand for 10 minutes. Serve warm with Kumquat Champagne Confit (page 236), and vanilla ice cream, if desired.

Kumquat Champagne Confit

This is a quick and tasty alternative to the more traditional marmalade recipe (page 96), and isn't meant to be canned. It comes together very fast and packs an incredible flavor. We love this on fresh baguettes with a nice soft cheese like brie or chèvre. It is also amazing as a topping for the Bread Pudding (page 234); just add a scoop of vanilla ice cream!

Makes 3 cups

1 cup sugar
2 cups champagne
1 cup water
1 star anise
25 kumquats, thinly sliced

1. In a medium-size saucepan, bring the sugar, champagne, water, and star anise to a simmer. Cook, stirring until sugar has dissolved.

2. Add the kumquats and gently simmer over medium-low heat until they are tender and the liquid is the consistency of thick maple syrup, about 20 minutes.

3. Use within 1 week.

Chocolate Cherry Bread Pudding

"There is no end to the combinations of flavors you can use to make bread pudding. This recipe was inspired by my family's annual vacation in Door County, Wisconsin, where we pick a bounty of fresh cherries. I first made this pudding with the Chocolate Bread (page 211). The intensity of the chocolate mixed with the tart cherries is a classic. It is also wonderful made with Brioche or Challah doughs, and dried cherries can be substituted when fresh are not available. Served with a premium-quality vanilla ice cream, this dessert will satisfy any chocolate craving."—Jeff

Makes 8 servings

3 cups half-and-half

¾ cup brown sugar

½ pound finely chopped high-quality bittersweet chocolate, preferably Valrhona or equivalent

¼ cup butter, cut in ½-inch slices

3 whole eggs

2 egg yolks

6 cups cubed day-old Chocolate Bread (page 211), Brioche (page 189), or Challah (page 180)

1½ cups pitted sour cherries

1. **Preheat the oven to 325°F.** Bring the half-and-half and brown sugar to a simmer.

2. Remove from heat and add the chocolate and butter to the half-and-half mixture, stirring until the chocolate is completely melted and smooth. Allow the mixture to cool slightly, about 5 minutes.

3. Whisk together the eggs and egg yolks and add to the cooled chocolate mixture.

4. Arrange the cubed bread and cherries in an 8×12×2-inch baking dish. Pour the chocolate custard over the bread and allow it to sit for 15 minutes. You may have to push the bread down into the custard to make sure it is well soaked.

5. Cover loosely with foil, poking a few holes in the top to allow steam to escape. Bake for about 50 minutes, or until the center is firm to the touch.

6. Allow to sit for 10 minutes before serving with vanilla ice cream.

INDEX

SOURCES FOR BREAD-BAKING PRODUCTS

Bob's Red Mill: www.bobsredmill.com, 800-349-2173

Hodgson Mill: www.hodgsonmill.com, 800-347-0105

King Arthur Flour: www.kingarthurflour.com/shop/, 800-827-6836

Penzeys Spices: www.penzeys.com, 800-741-7787

Tupperware: www.tupperware.com, 800-366-3800

Williams-Sonoma: www.williams-sonoma.com, 877-812-6235